A Garden of Visible Prayer

Creating a Personal Sacred Space
One Step at a Time

Margaret Rose Realy, Obl. OSB

Patheos Press
Denver, Colorado

Cover photo: *Tradescantia spathacea*, 'Sitara Gold' by Linda Stephens
Author photo copyright 2010 Thomas Gennara.

International Standard Book Number: 978-1-939221-23-0

Printed and bound in the United States of America.

Library of Congress Cataloging-in-Publication Data
Realy, Margaret Rose

A Garden of Visible Prayer, Creating a Personal Sacred Space One Step at a Time by Margaret Rose Realy, Obl. OSB

ISBN 978-1-939221-23-0 (pbk)

*This book is dedicated to
one fine and good Irishman,
Rev. Father Lawrence P. Delaney*

TABLE OF CONTENTS

PREFACE

A beginner must think of herself as one setting out to make a garden in which her Beloved Lord is to take his delight ... [1]

[1] Teresa of Avila, *The Book of My Life, Part Two, The Four Waters*. There are many translations available on St. Teresa's writings.

As an industrial and technological society, we are losing sight of what brings us solace and our memory of what is sacred. We are losing ourselves in the daily demands of working to stay working, and working in and on our homes. More importantly we are losing our memory of loved ones and our connectedness with God. Many people are also finding it increasingly difficult to find a place of inner peace that can lead to spiritual joy, strength and the energy to continue. We hunger to return to our place of origin with God, back to the garden, to rediscover that spiritual dimension of centering peace.

This book is a step-by-step approach to help guide you in creating a meaningful sacred space – a place you can step into, close at hand, matched to what brings you, personally, to inner quietness.

What I find when working with people who want to create a sacred space is that they don't know how to define what it is they seek or even where to begin. Some individuals surrender to the lack of direction by plopping down in a corner of their yard a bench with a container of annuals next to it and calling it good enough. Others spend a lot of money and several long hours developing a garden and find that, though beautiful by definition, their created landscape doesn't touch their spirit as they had hoped it would.

What happens in many situations is a random selection of elements that we like but that do not touch us spiritually. To develop a sense of place, it is important to find a way to identify what moves us. This is the time to look beyond our grandmother's garden or our neighbor's orderly plantings.

You may find that, much like decorating your home, a single item inspires you. You admire the color, shape, texture or memory it elicits. From this single item a sense of connection to the self comes alive. The "I like that" item cues us to contemplate what significance it holds for us.

In the book *Spiritual Gardening*, author Peg Streep states early on the importance of "tending to your inner landscape to foster the growth of your spirit."[2]

It is in quieting ourselves that the seed of God can enter into our fertile soil and lead us to bear the fruit he has purposely planted within us.

There are many inspiring books on the market that will help you in understanding the elements of landscape design and how certain aspects of a landscape affect us. A very brief overview of that information is included at the end of this book should you choose to look more deeply into what is available.

This book does not consider the need to landscape your whole yard, but only a very small portion of it so as to be able to attend to the landscape of your soul.

Let us begin the process in a step-by-step manner, to create a personalized garden of visible prayer.

[2] p. 11.

List of Supplies

The process of discerning your garden will require a few items from the office supply store. This activity is meant to be a physical endeavor, literally a hands-on experience. If you have a computer, you may find it to be of minimal use in this creative experience.

Essential supplies: a three-ring binder, tabbed dividers, a few pocket page protectors, notebook paper both lined and unlined, tracing paper, graph paper, crayons or colored pencils, lead pencils (with erasers), a few white address labels, scissors and a glue stick.

Nice to have: ruler, circle templates and a few sheets of assorted construction or scrapbooking paper.

As you work through this book, you can title each tab in your binder according to the chapters. Not all chapters will be applicable to your needs. Remember, this is your notebook and it is filled with information that leads you to create the prayer garden you desire. The later chapters will help you cull out and refine your collected ideas.

ACKNOWLEDGMENT

I feel a deep sense of gratitude to several friends for their efforts to bring this book into your hands.

With the encouragement and persistence of my editors, and there were several, these words written by a gardener have borne fruit as a book.

I am grateful to all the beloved volunteers who worked so patiently with me in the gardens at St. Francis Retreat Center, and listened to my starry-eyed ramblings of things to come. Through their encouragement this book was conceived.

To my dearest friend David and his family for keeping the faith as this book took on a life of its own. They always believed that God would provide whatever was needed to rebound to His own glory.

INTRODUCTION

I am a gardener and a Christian. It seems God is always close and speaks clearly to my heart whenever I seek him in a garden. I have always been involved with gardening and growing. Our family business was greenhousing, my maternal grandmother and I would garden together whenever we could and college started with botany and horticulture, though graduation came with a business degree.

Many years later when the economy plummeted, I sought the peace of gardening and growing once more. I had already completed the requirements for being an Advanced Master Gardener, so I studied and received

certification as a greenhouse grower and began working in the industry. As a landscape consultant, I helped many customers with questions and realized how hungry others were for the solace that could be found in a garden.

This sparked a growing awareness to combine the desire to serve God with the talent he had given me. I began creating prayer gardens at St. Francis Retreat Center in DeWitt, Michigan. Because of the size of this Center – 95 acres – the St. Francis Garden Society was created.

I prayed as I worked that others would find a way to come to the gardens. If they could quiet the din of daily life enough it would allow the gentle voice of God to be heard. I felt assured that the Holy Spirit would do the rest and bring them peace. As I planted and weeded at public gardens, church gardens and at the retreat center, visitors would let me know that my prayers were being answered.

The idea for this text came about because of the encouraging requests of those who found the peace of God in those simple gardens. Their wanting to know how to create their own sacred spaces led to small group discussions and then to classes where they were guided in the process of creating visible prayer. After presenting several workshops and numerous handouts for my participants, I wrote this book.

I pray that this book will help you to find a way to create either personal or public spaces for prayer. May the journey bring you closer to God. Because it is in our desire to find and please God that we indeed do so.

Veriditas: [L. green and truth] the "greening of the mind," the growth of intelligence and spiritual insight through encountering and understanding nature.

The great 12th century mystic, healer and philosopher, Hildegard von Bingen, created the word *veriditas* to describe her vision of the greening power of nature in gaining insight of the divine force of God within all life. It is her making of a synergistic concept in the Christian tradition that combines nature's manifest vitality and humankind's discernment of God.

Chapter 1

DEFINING THE GARDEN

"There are forces of the spirit that will help direct us if we can be still enough to listen and allow God to enter."[3]

When we say something is sacred, we usually mean that in some way it is consecrated to God, having to do with religion or that in some way it is venerated and hallowed. Spiritually dedicated gardens are those that attend to the interior need of our soul, heart and mind.

[3]Margaret Realy, *Lecture Series: God in the Garden.*

Gardens offer us a place where both plants and people can grow. We find all of our senses are engaged in a garden, even if we are impaired in some way. By creating a sacred space, we allow our spirit to grow in such a way that our interior landscape can reveal hidden hope.

A sanctuary is a place of refuge or protection and can be a building or a garden. It is a haven that we can return to that allows us to pray, to rejuvenate and to remember. What follows are some definitions of types of emotionally, physically and spiritually dedicated gardens.

Garden Types

Therapeutic gardens are part of a rehabilitation process that can support both mental and physical healing. Participants actively encounter or work in the garden to recover what they can of a lost skill. A horticultural therapist makes use of a garden of this type to address a medical concern and incorporate a recovery regimen. Most therapeutic gardens that are part of a medical or rehabilitation facility are public spaces with restricted access.

Healing gardens are very similar to therapeutic gardens with one key difference: the visitor to such a garden is not actively working with the physical environment. Healing gardens are more of an outdoor contemplative space. They are designed to lower physical and emotional stress and assist in personal renewal. This type of garden nurtures

the spirit while the body is healing. Many healing gardens are part of a medical or care facility and are usually public spaces, but can be private gardens. Just a small note – some herbal-centered medicinal or aromatherapy gardens are sometimes called healing gardens.

Meditative or prayer gardens are often used for spiritual centering, discernment and renewal. A garden of this nature may reflect the religion or philosophical belief system of the designer or visitors. Often times sacramental elements are present in the designs of these gardens. It is not uncommon for religious elements of prayer gardens to be incorporated into healing gardens as well. Prayer gardens can be both public and private spaces.

Memorial gardens are garden spaces specifically constructed to reflect or honor an individual, group or issue. Memorial gardens are meditative simply by their very purpose in focusing our attention on a particular issue. Again, these gardens can be both public and private spaces. *Chapter 2* is dedicated to creating this type of garden.

As you have probably figured out from these definitions, garden types easily overlap. Many of the concepts and most of the procedures addressed in this book can be applied to both public and private gardens. The type of garden you intend to create is loosely defined by how you intend to use it.

When conceptualizing your space, keep in mind whether it is to be a public garden being created for an organization or a private space for you or your family and friends. Your private garden will reflect what brings you, personally, to a centering peace. A public garden will be created for others, their desires and how they will use the space. When creating a public space, you should adhere to city and state codes. Do your homework and learn what these are before starting the installation.

Development of Intent

There are several questions to help you focus and put you in the best frame of mind for planning your prayer garden. Although these questions may seem simplistic and obvious, answer them nonetheless. Write your answers down ... this is the start of your notebook.

1. What are the reasons you visit a garden? Is it because you find it calming, you appreciate its aesthetic beauty, you like sharing time with others or God, or you want to reenergize yourself?

2. Why do you want to create a sacred space? Is it to find peace, escape from the din of daily life or find solitude?

3. Who is the subject of this garden? Is it for you? Is it a public space? Is it for someone who is deceased?

4. How will it be used? Is it to be a memorial, a retreat, a place to meditate? How will it function (i.e. a public space for baptisms, an extended sanctuary of a church or a place for outdoor worship)?

5. How will you or others occupy this space? Will you sit in it most of the time? Will you walk within it? Will you use it in the morning or at the gloaming of the day? Will you welcome other people into it?

6. Where will it be located? Behind the garage? Under a stand of pines? The vacant lot next to the church?

Look at your answers. Do you see a pattern of intent or purpose? Synonymous words should be present in your answers; circle them, rewrite them, pray over them. These intentions are your foundation.

The Look of Spirituality

Here you will identify the objects that would help put you in a frame of mind for prayer. In other words, what aspects of a garden induce a sense of spirituality for you?

Many years ago I attended a program about the history and creation of a spiritual landscape[4] and came away with many insights. One of the tools from that program that I still use is a form that I adapted and include here. You should begin with this form, too, and here is how to prepare it.

Take a sheet of paper and divide it into three columns. Write these headings across the top of the three columns:

Items | **Adjectives** | **Emotions**

Beginning in the *Items* column, list the elements you would likely find in a garden. Things like *water, birds, rocks, yellow flowers, blue gazing ball* ... just write down whatever comes to mind.

In the next column, *Adjectives*, write down characteristics or

---

[4]Dunbar, Dr. Frank, *Designing a Spiritual Landscape*, Hidden Lake Gardens, Tipton, Michigan, July 9, 2005.

descriptions of each item you wrote down in the first column. On example would be *rock … solid, still, unmoving; blue gazing ball … reflective, fragile*. Take your time to really think about what words describe the items in the first column.

The last aspect to consider is what *Emotions* are evoked by these items. This column takes a little more time, as well it should. Here you are identifying what feelings you want to nurture in your sacred space. Using the example of *rock … solid, still, unmoving* could evoke positive emotions of being *strong, dependable,* or negative ones of being *cold* and *hard*. These emotions will be different for each person. For example, I personally like large boulders in a garden, yet some of my clients have a real aversion to what they would describe as a hunk of stone lying around.

Remember that there is no right or wrong response in your list. No matter what you write in the last column, be honest with yourself. It will do you no good to try to please someone else with your answers. For example, a vivid orange flower might be beautiful to one person, but you really dislike that color. Or, if you are allergic to oranges, your true response would be a negative one.

Sample Table:

Items	Adjectives	Emotions
Rock	Solid, still, unmoving	Strong, secure
Blue gazing ball	Fragile, reflective	Contemplation
Tall grasses	Flowing, rapid growth, movement	Openness

Fragrance is a topic that deserves attention. In your table, draw a horizontal line under what you have previously written or start a new set of columns. You will add a new section and it will be called *Scents*. In the *Items* column list the scents you like and ones that stir your memory, and how they are evoked. Examples are *lilies by air movement, lavender by touch, alyssum by heat/air* and so on.

The *Adjectives* column is often more difficult to fill in with *Scents* because the other senses are not involved. Describing the characteristic of a fragrance is challenging to all but the most gifted of poets. Scent is a personal and very subjective aspect. For example, the Oriental Lily *Stargazer* can be described as both heavy and dizzying.

Because fragrances or aromas have a more powerful and direct psychological effect than the other senses, filling in the *Emotions* column is much easier.

Remember also to identify those scents that are not your favorites when considering a fragrance in your garden. A dear friend of mine develops severe headaches at the scent of spring hyacinths (*Hyacinth orientalis*). Another woman finds that the scent of paperwhite narcissus reminds her of her cat's litter box.

What negative associations, if any, do you have to certain fragrances? Make note of them in your table as well. Add the plant with a negative association in the *Items* column and include in the *Emotions* column a *red X*. You will want to avoid inadvertently adding those scents as your design progresses.

The last portion of your table is about colors. There is a section in *Chapter 6* dedicated to this aspect, but for now identifying the emotions that certain colors evoke is our purpose here. Again, draw another horizontal line or start a new set of columns labeled *Colors*, and fill in each column accordingly as you work across the chart.

If you had a big box of Crayola Crayons,™ you may remember that the colors were labeled in very creative ways – names like Carnation Coral, Aztec Gold and Jungle Green. They definitely inspired a response and often made me smile. Remember that in a garden, green is more than the background. It, too, is a color and there are a lot of shades of green to be considered. It is the subtleties of color that will help you discover what inspires your spirit.

Focusing your Inspirations

This concluding step will help narrow your vision on what you need as well as what you want in your garden. Look closely at your tables, especially the *Emotions* column, and circle the responses that point you in the direction of your desired outcome for a prayer space.

Even though when you look at the *Emotions* column you see a lot of feelings, circle only those that best fit the intent of your space as designated in the first part of this chapter. If you intend to use your space to invigorate your life, words like "moving" or "delight" should be circled. Should your space be designed as a quiet retreat, than your designated words would be "calming" or "reflective."

Travel from right to left in your table, from the *Emotions* that you have circled to the associated *Items*. Here are the basic building blocks for your space – highlight those items, then select one of those items as the focal point of your meditative or prayer space. It could be a wrought iron piece of art shaped like a cross, a silver gazing ball or a clump of 'Karley Rose' (*Pennisetum orientale* 'Karley Rose') ornamental grass. This meditative item will be the last element you will install in your garden.

You have now completed a crucial step in defining your sacred space. You have identified your intention of how you will use this space, what emotions you want to evoke and what objects will fulfill those needs.

The next set of chapters is simply the "plug-and-play" of designing. The hardest part is done.

Chapter 2

MEMORIAL GARDENS

"We can help transform an inner darkness by creating outer beauty."[5]

[5]*Midwest Living*, p. 107.

This is a very brief chapter with a very specific focus. Memorial gardens are garden spaces specifically constructed to reflect or honor an individual, group or issue. Memorial gardens are meditative simply by their very purpose of focusing our attention on an individual or event.

There is a great deal more freedom in creating a personal memorial garden for, let's say, your dad, than there would be in creating a public space to honor soldiers or a notable person. Public spaces must be designed with the needs of others kept in mind. The exercises in the previous chapter can still be used with added attention placed on which elements evoke appropriate responses associated with the intended memorial within the community where it is placed.

The key here is identifying the culture of the community who will be using the space. A memorial suited to the culture and style of a Middle Eastern community will be very different from one for a predominantly Polish neighborhood.

At this stage, be very open about potential images and concepts. Remember, you are constructing a notebook, so enter the written answers to the following questions into it. Refining them will come later.

When designing a memorial or prayer garden for a community, the following questions should be answered:

1. What process is needed to create the garden? (This is a simple step-by-step project management plan working backwards from the completion date. It would include such things as permits, land grant

titles, materials acquisition list and the dates they are due for the project to continue in a timely manner.)

2. What elements should be included based on cultural association? (Elements used for a Catholic Hispanic community are not the same those you would use for Japanese Catholics.)

3. What images and potential symbolism will reflect the sacred for this cultural group?

4. What site location will fit the sacred space? (Be sure to consider exposure to sun and wind, the view from outsiders and potential distractions.)

When considering a person to be memorialized with a garden or whether the space will be private or public, the questions are the same:

1. Who is the memorial garden about: the person or the family?

2. What is it that he or she loved? Or did? What was his or her favorite color or object?

3. What is it that you or a community loved about him or her?

Sometimes a memorial garden will include an object that is very special and specific to the person. If your brother was a fireman, you may have a statue of a Dalmatian tucked in beside the red petunias. This is fine and very endearing in a private space. But such overt references in a public space will detract from the overall essence and design.

Take this information about the intent of the memorial garden and create a table as you did in *Chapter 1*.

You will find it much easier to create your table when a memorial to a loved one is being designed. You already have a great deal of emotional information available.

Whether it is a memorial garden you want to design, or some other type, you will need to think about some essential components and that is what we will look at in the next chapter.

Chapter 3

COLLECTING IDEAS

"I marvel at how being unsure of a situation is not a bad thing. Rather, it opens us to being observant and allows us to seek the portal within, guiding us to our own creative flow."[6]

When designing your sacred garden, it should contain the elements you identified in your table. You now have a pretty good idea of what is reflective of your spirituality and will move you closer to God. Your table also reflects a recurring theme that, with a discerning heart, you have identified.

[6]Nancy Endres, *Midwest Living Magazine*, The Healing Garden, August 2005, p. 108.

There are certain essential elements to any garden. You will collect images reflecting the items that you had identified as your personal essential elements, such as wrought iron gate or rocks.

In this chapter we begin the process of making a wish list for your garden by collecting ideas and images. And you will probably collect a lot of them. Magazines are your best tool. Those that deal with the home, gardens and travel are usually the most helpful.

The Internet is also an amazing resource for images. Using a search engine, you can select images for a set of words you enter and pull up thousands of pictures – some of them not even set in gardens but ones that will convey an emotion. Unless you are fairly good at narrowing your search, you could get lost in the results. I find that being fairly specific and viewing only the first three or so pages of results from an Internet search prevents your wasting time wandering around the Web.

The main purpose of seeking a collection of images for your garden's design is that it helps you to identify visually what you find pleasing. Look carefully at the images you have collected. A theme, much like what you found with your table, will begin to emerge from of your collection.

If you find an image that has a lot of interest to it but you only are drawn to one element, post a note on the clipping next to the feature stating what drew you to it. Maybe it's the shape of a tree, or the line of a bench – whatever it is, make note. Otherwise, when you go back and look at your clippings you may have no idea why you saved that picture from *Travel and Leisure* of a hillside scene in Quebec.

Remember the pocket page protectors I suggested in the list of supplies? Here is where you will use them.

Mark the lower right-hand corner of each pocket with a white label that contains the heading of the essential or personal element you plan to incorporate into your garden. A list of what are *Essential Elements* and *Personal Elements* follows this section (you may not plan on using all of them, so only designate pockets for those elements that you like). Then place these pockets in your binder.

As you clip or print out images (a wonderful pastime in nongardening months), place the images inside the appropriate pocket. In a surprisingly short time you will begin to see your preferences form a style as the collection grows.

You will notice that we are giving very little attention right now to the actual plants that will be in the garden. You may have pictures of plants that attract you and by all means save them. But the final plant selection process is a detailed activity discussed in *Chapter 9*.

Essential Elements

Transition Element

This is a feature that designates the beginning or end of a garden. It cues you to alter your frame of mind because you are entering a different space. A transition element also can signify a sacred garden space within a larger garden. The element could include but is not limited to gates, arbors and steps. Plantings can also indicate a transition as can containers that are strategically placed. The term "transition" has other meanings in landscape architecture, but for our purpose here this definition will be sufficient.

Dividers

These are visual barriers that create a sense of enclosure in a prayer garden, like a row of tall grasses or a large container on a deck. Dividers are not for everybody. Some people may prefer a vista that is open to the eye and opens up the heart. Dividers can be part of the transition element or a stand-alone feature. They can be made of constructed materials or privacy plantings.

Seating

This can include benches, tables with chairs or any arrangement you desire. Having a back to rest against is always nice if you intend to sit in your garden for a while. If you plan to share your space with others, be sure to include seating for them nearby. You may want to include a small table where you can write or set down a drink or book.

My personal preference is seating for two. This preference comes from a story told to me by a priest about one of his peers who had gone to the house of a woman who was caring for her elderly and dying father. As the priest entered the bedroom to visit with the gentleman, the older man asked him to sit on the end of the bed instead of the chair that he was approaching.

The older man told the priest that the chair next to his bed was for Christ, whom he talked to from time to time. He asked that his daughter not be told, because she might think him addled and silly. So through all his visits the priest sat on the edge of the bed and never mentioned it to her.

A short time later, the daughter called very distraught. Her father had passed away and she had found him half fallen out of bed. She was grieved to think that her dad was trying to get up and she had not heard him. When he questioned the daughter at the wake, the priest learned that her father had his head and arms in the chair by his bed when she found him. At this, the priest shared with her what the old man had shared with him. The priest knew that her father had died resting his head in the lap of Christ, who sat in the chair next to his bed.

For me, not only in my room, but in my garden as well, there will always be a second chair.

Walkways

These can be as formal or as simple as you choose. They are best when curved in casual settings, but if you like a formal garden space, then use straight lines. Be aware that straight lines and angles invigorate the senses because they create visual tension. As you collect images of the type of materials you like – such as stone, grass or mulch – the line you prefer for your walkway will become clearer.

Shade

Sitting in the sun for an extended period of time can be uncomfortable and unhealthful. Unless you are planning a night garden as a sacred space, it will be important that you factor in a means for shade. One of the quickest ways to provide shade when none is available is with a divider trellis placed behind a bench.

Water Feature

This element is probably the most often used as a focal point in any garden setting. It provides visual interest, sound, movement and water for the fauna of the area. A water feature can be as simple as a shallow piece of ceramic tucked into the ground or as elaborate as a waterfall and pool. Keep your budget in mind as you cut out pictures. For now, maybe a fountain in the shape of a small urn will suffice until you can afford installing a reflective pond with Koi.

Color

The emotive and physical responses to color are as varied as there are hues. There is section on color in *Chapter 6* that discusses color in more detail. For now, focus on pictures that coincide with the information revealed from the table you developed in *Chapter 1*.

Generally speaking, calming colors are at the blue end of the spectrum, invigorating colors at the red/yellow end. Pastels are more soothing than richly saturated colors. Look for color in plants as well as in hardscape pieces – benches, dividers, etc.

Anchor Points

These would be elements that draw attention. Anchor points are sometimes called focal points. They include things like art, sacramental items, water features, a vista and so on. In landscape architectural terms, "Focal points are places that draw your eye, that cause you to focus for a moment during a visual sweep of a scene, that even orient you in that direction."[7] In a general sense, everything you clip out and save for your pockets has a point of interest, an item in it that drew your attention. What you will be doing here will be to collect images that will let you focus reflectively while in a small sacred space.

[7]Janet Macunovich, *Designing Your Gardens and Landscapes*, p. 28.

Habitat

This has to do with the fauna in your area – birds, deer, butterflies or squirrels. Look for pictures of elements that will draw these creatures into your space – or keep them out of it – things like a hummingbird water station, deer-deterrent fencing, bird houses or feeders. You get the idea.

Plants

As you collect images of plants or illustrations of planting designs, keep in mind that these pictures will guide you in the final stage of plant selection. Remember that Martha Stewart does not live at your house, and few if any gardens really look like the magazine photo for more than a couple of hours.

Personal Elements

These are the part of your sacred outdoor space not usually considered essential to a garden. Yet they are reflective of a singular element you may want included.

Memory Images

In *Chapter 2* on *Memorial Gardens* I mentioned that items that were reflective or familiar to the individual could be used – sparingly – in a private garden, and very cautiously in a public space. Your collection of pictures will by its nature be specific to whom or what is being memorialized.

Verses and Quotations

These need to be very concise, easy to read and appropriate to the theme of the space. One of my favorite activities in creating public prayer spaces is to imprint a short verse in the cement platform for seating by using a cement lettering kit.[8] These kits can be purchased on-line, through garden gift catalogs. Occasionally they can be found in retail stores.

There is a lot of information contained in this chapter about the things you want to include in your garden. Let yourself loose to collect an abundance of images to fill the pocket pages in your binder. You will find a theme and a personal style emerge as you progress. In *Chapter 8* we will begin the process of culling them to best fit your desires for your prayer garden.

[8]Poetry Stone Deluxe Kit, Magnetic Poetry, Inc., Minneapolis, MN.

Chapter 4

PRAYER GARDEN LOCATION

"The truest silence is interior: an attentive receptivity ... We need only stop our mental chatter ..."[9]

[9]Rev. Nancy Roth, *Organic Prayer: Cultivating Your Relationship with God*, p.76.

If you have a very small yard, as I do, the location of your prayer space may already be evident and require only that you make the best of it. For those of you who have options, here are a few recommendations.

Your first consideration is when you will use the space and the orientation of the sun. What hour of the day will you spend time in your private retreat? Will it be early mornings in preparation for heading out for the day? Mid-afternoon before the kids come home from school? After work? Because it can be very uncomfortable and unhealthful sitting in the sun for an extended period of time, plan to create shade if none exists during that time.

If you plan to use your sacred space as a contemplative area, consider a quieter location away from distractions. If your focus is prayer and meditation about your family, have your house as the focal point from where you sit. If you will use your sacred space as a quick break in a busy day, make it easily accessible.

One of the most endearing and easily accessible prayer spaces I have ever encountered was created by a busy mom of meager means. She found a large rectangular trellis at a yard sale and attached it to the edge of the roof that hung over a cement slab porch. Heavenly Blue Morning Glories (*Ipomoea tricolor* 'Heavenly Blue') were planted in hand-painted pastel pots and grew up the trellis. She moved her garden Madonna statue into this space and placed it on a matching inverted pot. Recycling some old brick, she created a twelve-inch fire pit for incense and tossed down

some old cushions that she had covered in tablecloths from the resale store. The sacred space was close at hand, quiet, reflected her faith and incorporated those elements that led her to prayer.

Decks offer a variety of opportunities for prayer space. The deck area can be divided into "rooms" much like the living spaces in a house. A corner of the deck will give more privacy than the center, and by using tall grasses in containers you can create a transition point or divider. Don't forget about the space beside the deck next to the house. This 90° corner has great potential because it offers a ready-made enclosed space nearby.

Other places that offer sheltered nooks are under or beside trees, by an existing trellis or arbor in your yard, or in spaces between the house and garage.

My first prayer garden made use of the narrow piece of lawn between the house and a six-foot stockade fence. After finally settling into the new house, and having done my homework all winter, I stepped out ready to create my garden early that first spring. This private little garden was quickly completed: narrow flower beds, shade from an old apple tree, cushioned chairs, twig table and cement cherubs sitting on shelves created on the back of the fencing. Visually and spiritually pleasing, this prayer garden was small enough to evoke a sense of enclosure and to stimulate the senses. So don't hesitate to make that small side yard, the space behind the garage or that shadowed corner next to the shed beautiful.

Although that first prayer garden seemed ideal, I would like to share my mistake in hopes of preventing someone else from making the same error. It became obvious as that first summer rolled around that I had not adequately anticipated noise from the street. There were motorcycles and trucks with loud mufflers, motor homes rumbling along, and car loads of vacationers with blaring radios – all making their way to the lake along the main road where I now lived. It is a very pretty garden, but useless for contemplation.

As you look at different areas in your yard, imagine a line perpendicular to the side of the house, outbuilding, fence or retaining wall. Drop an imaginary line using these structures, a tree or the side of a slope as a corner. Just imagine the possibilities for a private space … and now get a lawn chair.

Use the tried and true process of a lawn chair placed at different spots in your yard to determine where you will sit in your garden. Once you find a view or nook you like, leave the chair there for a few days. Look at the chair from inside the house. Does its location seem compatible with the view out your window? If you continue to gravitate to this spot when you're outdoors, you will have found your garden site.

Take a few photos of your lawn chair as it sits where your garden will be. Looking directly at the chair and standing a short distance away, take one picture each of the following: directly in front of the chair, standing behind it and from each side. When it is time to draw your garden design, you will have a view from different angles to work with. Paste your pictures onto a sheet of notebook paper, write on this same page any observations and notes about your chosen location and add the sheet to your binder.

Look also at your desired location during different times of the day and make notes. When is it in full sun? Does it stay damp too long in the morning or after a rain? Is that where the dog usually relieves itself? Note also what plants currently exist and, if they are suitable, how you can incorporate them into your design.

When you have decided where your garden will be located and some of its characteristics, it will be time to start assessing the site.

Chapter 5

SITE ASSESSMENT

A sacred space is a place for remembering not only 'who we are, but whose we are'. It is a space where seeds of quiet can enter in and grow Grace.[10]

The site assessment involves gathering information on the physical nature of your chosen garden area. There a few things to take into consideration after you have selected the location for your prayer space. As you work through each, make your final notes on the sheet that has the picture of your chair. We are working with a very small portion of your landscape so your assessment will be narrow and very focused.

Your site assessment will directly affect the plant selection for your garden. If you already have a garden in place and are only sectioning off a portion of it as a retreat area, then this chapter will provide you with an overview. Do make notes of your existing garden, for you may have an inclination to adjust the plantings to match your new awareness of a sacred space.

Sunlight and Shade

You will want to know how many hours during the
day that direct sunlight rests on your location. Generally

defined, full sun equals six or more hours, partial sun equals four to six hours, shade equals about two to four hours, and dense shade either receives no direct sunlight or only up to two hours. Keep a small pad of paper handy and check your location at different times during the day.

Notice the term *"direct sunlight"* – this is unobstructed sunlight directly resting on a plant's leaves. Shade is altered or diffused sunlight. In your small garden you will probably have more than one kind of shade. An example would be a prayer space with a trellis divider next to where you sit creating dappled shade, while at the same time there is a tree that blocks all sunlight at the end of your garden. Types of shade are defined as follows:

Dense Shade

No direct sunlight or two hours or less of it; includes heavy tree canopy and the north sides of buildings. Dense shade, as indicated above, completely blocks any rays of sun getting to the ground or only allows for a very brief period of sunlight. Many of you are familiar with walking in dense woodlands, or entering a tunnel like space where branches intersect over a path. But dense shade can also describe that difficult section of yard between your house and your neighbor's garage. Another thing that may occur in this corridor-like space is that the only two hours of sunlight that do permeate the space could be mid- to late-afternoon, and this direct sunlight tends to burn the life right out of shade plants.

Full or Afternoon Shade

Six or more hours of solid shade. It includes the east side of a structure or high slope and is oftentimes referred to as "morning sun only." Morning sun is not as intense as that of mid-day or afternoon. A spot receiving morning sun followed by afternoon shade is preferred for plants that require partial shade.

Medium Shade

Four to six hours of shade and includes high shade. High shade allows bright, reflective sunlight into an area. This happens when tree branches are trimmed up high on the trunk and reflected light is available from things like siding, water or cement. Plants often respond to this type of shade as though they were in light shade even though direct sunlight is absent. A lot of times high shade and dappled are seen together.

Dappled or Light Shade

Three to four hours of shade is considered light shade. Dappled shade is sunlight between the leaves that moves throughout the day, as on a lawn. Some sun-loving plants will survive but not thrive in this environment.

This may be a lot more information on shade than you wanted to know, but keep these terms in mind when your planting list begins to develop.

Soil

For many home gardeners, this topic causes the "deer in the headlights" kind of response. I will discuss some general terms very briefly and help you to quickly identify your soil type. There are many excellent reference books on the market about soils and how to amend them, if you decide to expand your knowledge and gardening skills.

Start by looking around your site and seeing what plants grow and their overall conditions. Weeds are a very good indicator of soil type. Well-groomed lawns are not good indicators of soil conditions because they are often watered and fertilized instead of being self-supporting. Also look at the general condition of plants growing in the surrounding area and note which ones are thriving or spindly. This will help you determine your own soil's condition.

Listed below are a few basic definitions of soil conditions:

Soil Texture

This is determined by the relative portions of sand, silt and clay. It is an inherent soil property of the area you live in. Texture influences the soil's properties such as drainage. With a little effort the texture of a small area of soil can be altered. You can improve the soil of a garden with amendments such as peat and compost.

Tilth

The physical condition of the soil as it relates to ease of

seeding, emergence and root penetration. Essentially, this is the soil's ability to support plants. You can improve the tilth of soil by improving its texture.

Compaction

This means that the soil particles have been mechanically pressed together to the point of nearly eliminating the spaces for air and water movement. This creates a condition known as hard pan. Think of a dirt driveway – no amount of tilling will return this hard compacted soil to a cultivatable condition. It has lost its tilth.

You can do a simple check of the soil at your site by digging a six-inch deep hole, which is the depth of most spades, picking up a handful of the soil and lightly squeezing it. You are looking for the amount of moisture being retained. Obviously, if it has just rained, wait a couple of days for the soil to drain before doing this test.

When you squeeze the soil, is it really dry and crumbly (sandy)? Is it cool and slightly damp while holding together (loam)? Or is it heavy and somewhat gooey (clay)?

To further assess soil texture, a quick and well-known method uses a quart jar, water and soil. As the particles of soil separate, they will naturally sort themselves out by weight and will create layers: heavy sand will be at the bottom of the jar, medium-weight silt will be in the middle, and lighter clay at the top (although sometimes if clay is very fine and light it may float making the water appear cloudy).

The relative proportions of these layers help you see what type of soil you have.

Procedure for Soil Structure Analysis

1. Take a soil sample from a few six-inch deep holes dug at the site location. Remove debris, mix together and break up any lumps. Then measure out one cup of soil.

2. Get a quart jar with a lid.

3. Put the cup of soil in the bottom of the jar, fill the jar full of water to within ½ inch from the top, add only a couple of drops of dish soap, and screw on the lid tightly.

4. Shake the living daylights out of the jar. Make sure all particles are thoroughly separated.

5. Set the jar aside in a location where it won't get bumped during the next 24 hours.

6. Get a ruler and hold it against the side of the jar. Begin measuring the sediments:
   a. After one minute, measure and record the number of inches of the settled particles of sand.
   b. After an hour, measure and record the depth of the soil, subtracting the level of sand recorded. This is silt.
   c. After 24 hours, measure the level and subtract the two previous numbers. This is the clay.
   d. Calculate the percentage: Divide the depth of each layer by the total depth of soil, and then multiply by 100.[11]

A relatively equal portion of sand and silt particles with a little clay is considered loam. This type, and sandy loam where you have a bit more sand than silt in your jar, are usually the best types for gardening. If you have a noticeable amount of clay, don't fret. There are plants that do well in clay and other plants that are called "clay-busters."

A small caveat here: just because your soil structure is hard and doesn't drain does not necessarily mean it is

[11] Taylor's Guide, Gardening Techniques, p. 47-48.

clay. Compacted soil that has lost its tilth has the same characteristics. Compacted soil will not separate out into three layers. In either situation – clay or compaction – planting a garden in that location is not your best option and you will need to give way to using containers.

We have discussed the soil's structure. To determine the chemical make-up of your soil, a soil sample will need to be analyzed. This can be done through your county's extension office, landscape firms or any number of soil testing services. The soil analysis will tell you the pH level and percentages of other chemicals and trace elements present. This information will help you determine plant selection and possible fertilizing needs.

Water Source

A garden hose that can be dragged to your area is probably the most you will have to consider. If you have an in-ground watering system you may need to have the heads adjusted. Of course, if you plan on locating your prayer space at the back of forty acres, watering will be an issue.

Also be sure to consider how long the area remains wet or dry after a rain. The lack of water on a dry site will be a factor in how much time you will need to set aside to attend to the garden. If you have located your space in a sandy area, at the top of a slope, under the eaves of the house or under a lot of maple trees, you can be sure that the area will most likely be dry. To accommodate this type of soil, you could select drought-tolerant plants, amend the soil, use mulch to help hold more moisture and plan to water regularly.

A yard that is in a low-lying area or one with a high water table would also create drainage problems. If the area is damp, look where the downspouts are located if you are near a building. Can you reroute the downspouts, add a curved portion or extend it? Obviously a wet area is not an appropriate location for a garden if you plan to sit in it, although it may make a very nice rain garden to look at.

Exposure

In landscape architecture, this has more to do with heat and sun, wind and frost. Though these are all factors to be considered in your garden as a whole, for our purposes we want to narrow the definition and look at how your site ensures that it will be a contemplative experience and will minimize distractions, both physically and mentally.

We have already mentioned how the sun and its heat are unhealthful and can make you uncomfortable in your prayer space. This exposure is easily managed with shade. If you do not have a tree or a building to provide shade, creating it can be easily accomplished. The simplest is a patio umbrella. For a more dramatic look consider creating an awning-like structure of cloth called a shade sail. For full sun exposure on a deck, a retractable awning is an option. Installing a pergola or arbor to sit under will also give a sense of being in a room, and attaching a bench-style swing provides a place to rock while resting.

Remember my story in an earlier chapter of my first

privacy garden? It was very exposed to street noise. For your own garden, keep this in mind and the recreational activities that may take place nearby. A prayer garden on the other side of a garage that has a basketball hoop attached would not prove to be very relaxing if the kids are home.

Privacy and proximity to others is an important factor here. Do you want to be able to see others if they come into your yard or approach the side door? Would you rather feel you are secluded? How private do you want your sacred space to be?

If you plan to use your space at night, be sure to consider intrusive light sources such as porch or flood lights and street lights. For safety while you walk around your garden, or maybe reading, you may want to plan for some low-level lighting at night.

Roots

Some of us may be blessed to have shade trees in our yards. Their roots will prove challenging when creating a garden space but try to prevent damaging them too much when digging.

Laying ground cloth over the exposed root knees and spreading mulch around them is an excellent way to create a sitting area. Large containers are always a nice touch under shade trees. Adding an arbor or some type of divider around this space would create the sense of being in a small room.

As you are assessing your site, write down your observations and add them to your binder.

There are only a few more steps before beginning the design.

Chapter 6

OUR SENSES

"There is a further kind of prayer nourishment ... which we can receive from the earth through our senses."[12]

Our physical senses can help deepen our awareness of a garden and assist in leading us to meditation and prayer. Sounds, sight, fragrances and, to a lesser extent, touch, are all part of the garden experience.[13] As you read this chapter, make notes about how each sense can be personally experienced in your space.

[12]Rev. Nancy Roth, *Organic Prayer: Cultivating Your Relationship with God,* p. 65.
[13]The fifth sense of taste does not really fit into the aspect of visible prayer, even though the taste of a fresh peach is considered by some to be divine.

Sounds, Created and Organic

Sounds take on a unique quality when we are being contemplative: the sounds of nature, the sounds of water, the sounds of a city, the sounds of our family. We may desire to be receptive to some sounds in our prayer space. Other sounds we may want to minimize.

Sounds can be organic or created. Simply put, the sounds of nature such as birds, wind and crickets are organic. Water is also considered organic and can be manipulated to vary its intensity and type of sound. We can create sounds in our garden with wind chimes or have intrusive created sounds from cars and kids.

When introducing a sound into your space, ask yourself how the sound affects you mentally and spiritually. One client intentionally tosses hard-shelled nuts to the squirrels in her yard. She delights in watching the squirrels scurry onto a branch and hearing them crunching away. Yet another friend is completely distracted and compulsively distressed by any sounds of chewing.

Nature produces a cacophony of sounds, some of which you can manipulate. I enjoy the sounds of birds singing and chirping when I am in a garden. I do not enjoy the shrill whistle from a cardinal right over my head or the screech of an irritated blue jay. To direct my avian friends elsewhere, I place the birdbath, houses or feeders (with the exception of those for hummingbirds) at some distance from where I sit.

Sounds from water vary in type and intensity. With

moving water, the faster the flow over rocks or the higher the fall from the edge of a fountain, the more noticeable the sound will be. If your spiritual elements include a fountain, the flow and fall of water is what you will hear. A pool or pond of still water may have just the soft sound of a bird bathing or a frog plopping into it.

From your table in *Chapter 1*, what had you identified that you liked about water? Was it trickling and soft or flowing and distinct? Had you found that a still pool was more suited to your needs or a gurgling fountain more to your liking?

For some individuals the sound of water is distracting. An attendee at one of my programs shared with others in the group her sense that running water meant washing dishes, and she always felt compelled to get up and do her housework. For another participant, a garden design that included a fountain had to be changed because the lady of the house had "bladder issues" at the sound of water. Obviously, neither of these women found spirituality when they sat next to flowing water.

There are other sounds to consider that could affect your contemplative area. Some cannot be avoided, such as, in my situation, the noise of cars and trucks on a busy road. For a friend who lives near Detroit, it is the sounds of jets from the airport a short distance away. Do you live next to a playground or school? Is there a railroad crossing a few blocks away? Many of us are fortunate enough that we do not have to deal with these issues where we live.

If you do have sounds that you want to minimize, try locating your garden space as far from the source as possible and install a succession of sound-absorbing plantings to reduce some of the noise. Tall Arborvitae (*Thuja spp.*) work very well. So do taller ornamental grasses. Deaden the sound bouncing off a building by buffering its reflective wall surface. Inside a house you would use drapes and carpeting to deaden the sound. In your garden, you could use a line of sound-absorbing plants as mentioned previously, trellised plants or hang wicker mats.

Sight, Visual Interests and Color

Visually pleasing landscape design incorporates several elements: mass, form, repetition, line and texture, to name just a few. If you have property that is landscaped, you will want to be sensitive to how your prayer space fits into the whole of your yard.

In this workbook, we will take a myopic view of your space. For a more thorough understanding of these and additional concepts of design, check the Internet or refer to the reference books listed in the *Annotated Bibliography* at the end of this book.

The anchor or focal point were mentioned earlier and you noted what your desired element of visual interest would be. As a reminder, you could have selected a water feature, sacramental object, rocks or maybe the view of your home as the focal point for prayer.

Color is very influential in a prayer space. The spiritual associations of color are personal, expansive and cultural. Colors can evoke memories and associations.

A favorite green in the garden and one that I use often is the soft blue-green leaves of sage (*Salvia officinalis*) and lavender (*Lavendula spp.*). I spent a lot of time with my maternal grandmother and this was the color on most of the walls in her house. As an adolescent in Detroit when the race riots erupted, the calming affect of being in her home during those turbulent times is a memory that reminds me to be still and trust in the general goodness of others.

With pencil and paper at hand as you go through an overview of color, make note about what memories or feelings come to the surface. "Truly seeing color in the spiritual garden reminds us that our range of perception is broader than our range of expression."[14] You may not have the exact words to express why a color is more personal for you. What matters is that the feelings evoked by a color meet the desired response for your prayer space.

Color Wheel

A circular diagram in which primary and usually intermediate colors are arranged sequentially so that related colors are next to each other and complementary colors are opposite. Even though this is more of a design issue, it seems important to address how groupings of colors affect the emotions in the space you are planning.

Here is a basic reminder of some terminology. In the color wheel, the first three colors are the primary ones from which all other colors are created.

Primary Colors

There are three: yellow, red and blue. Primary colors evoke more intense feelings.

Secondary Colors

There are three here also, orange, purple, and green. These colors tend to blend the emotions of the primary colors. An example is where yellow, which is intense and brings excitement, is combined with blue, which is reflective and detached, to create green which tends to discourage intensity of focus and brings you to a sense of restfulness.

Tertiary Colors

There are six resulting from the combination of primary and secondary colors, such as blue-green, red-orange and so on. These complete the twelve-part color wheel. Like secondary colors, tertiary colors, too, are a blending of feelings that the combined colors convey.

Harmonious or Analogous Colors

These are any two to four colors that are side by side on a twelve-part color wheel, such as yellow-green, yellow

---

[14]Peg Streep, *Spiritual Gardening: Creating Sacred Space Outdoors*, p. 33.

and yellow-orange. One of the three colors is usually predominating visually, such as the orange of Pot Marigold (*Calendual officinalis* 'Fiesta Gitana') and is accented by other harmonious colors such as red-orange day lilies (*Hemerocallis spp.*) and yellow-orange Signet Marigold (*Tangetes signata* 'Pumila'). Harmonious color combinations often convey a sense of peace – of being in harmony.

Complimentary Colors

Any two colors directly opposite each other on a color wheel, such as red and green or red-purple and yellow-green, are complimentary. These opposing colors create maximum contrast and stability or balance. They create a sense of excitement, give drama and add tension.

Take a moment and recall the purpose of your sacred space. Did you want to create a sense of excitement and revitalizing energy (complimentary colors) or a sense of release to find calm (harmonious colors)?

Monochromatic

This is a single color hue in a range of tints (moving toward pastels) and shades (moving toward darker tones). A garden all in blues would be considered monochromatic. Similar to a harmonious garden, it not only uses the colors next to each other on the color wheel, it also includes lighter and darker hues.

The emotional energy of the garden will depend on the color choice. If you want to feel invigorated in your garden, use red-oranges, orange, peach, tangy yellow. If you want to feel calm, use blues, grays and silver.

It is hard to create a monochromatic garden but when done well the results can be very elegant. Be careful though: monochromatic gardens can often be seen as indulgent, fall into the realm of garish when using bright colors or appear muddied if using darker ones.

Polychromatic

This includes a riot of colors that creates a festive and party-like feel to a garden. This color scheme is often used in children's gardens and memorials.

Cool Colors

Theses are at the green-blue-violet end of the spectrum and are more soothing and calming than reds and yellows. Cool colors appear to blend and seem to disappear when seen at a distance and so should be used for viewing up close.

Warm Colors

These are at the yellow-orange-red end of the spectrum and are more invigorating and exciting than cool colors. These give an impression of warmth and stand out when looked at from a distance.

Green

This is the most abundant color in the garden. The virtue of hope is symbolized by green and represents growth, fertility, renewal, harmony, tranquility, restfulness and balance. It is an alluring and enticing color in that it can make us pause and mentally "breathe" before we are even conscious we need to do so.

Blue

Blue leads us to the infinite world beyond. Blue is contemplative and cooling. It represents sky and water. It directs our perspective outwards – a looking beyond. Blue is used to calm and relax and encourages openness, communication and prayer.

Purple

This is a meditative color, a color of purpose. It combines the calmness, coolness and expansiveness of blue with the focus and energy of red. It is a creative color we associate with inspiration.

Red

Red is the warmest of all colors and symbolizes energy, intensity and fiery passion. It is extroverted activity, vitality, strength and prosperity. Dark burgundy reds represent mystery. It is the opposite of blue in the emotive spectrum. Because of the amount of energy in the color red, use it very sparingly in a contemplative garden.

Orange

A primary characteristic of this color is to enhance curiosity and exploration. It is indicative of change, a dynamic of thoughtful change rather than the explosive nature of red and suggests increased creativity and energy.

Yellow

Yellow is pure, bright and the easiest of all colors to see. It is full of intellectual energy, symbolizing wisdom, joy, happiness, attentiveness and illumination. It brings awareness and clarity to the mind.

White

White is the color of the Holy Spirit, of truth and sanctity. It represents purity, innocence and kindness. I read somewhere that white teaches us about relationships because, in our perceptions of colors, it tints how we see. White is in itself not a color but the complete revealed energy (manifestation) of all the colors – a very nice explanation of the completeness of the Holy Spirit. Use ten percent white in your garden to make other colors stand out.

Black

Black is perceived as mysterious, suggesting possibility. In Gestalt psychology black is the void that is full of hidden potential. Like white, it is in itself not a color, but the absorption of all colors. It conceals them. It usually does not work well in shaded areas. Use black sparingly, as an accent, and plant this color up close for viewing.

Gray

Gray is the color of emptiness, a lack of movement and emotion. It conveys restfulness, maturity and security. It will stabilize other, more vibrant colors. Gray or silver-leaved plants give the eye a place to rest in the garden.

Pastels

These are lighter tones (tints of white) and impart a softening and calming of the main color. Pastels, like most warm colors, will help draw light into deeply shaded areas.

Saturated/Vibrant

More saturated colors are also considered bold or vibrant and tied to stronger emotions, while unsaturated ones are softer and less striking. Strong sun light can visually wash out softer colors. Highly saturated and intense colors, including richer greens, work best in full sun gardens viewed during midday.

Fragrance

Our sense of smell can focus our attention immediately. Fragrance can be overt and intoxicating as in the scent of Stargazer lilies (*Lilium* 'Stargazer') or as subtle as the smell of freshly-turned soil. Scents can create emotions that are on the surface of our psyches or elicit memories that we have repressed. Scent is universal, but what a person considers fragrant is very personal.

How will you plan to incorporate this sense in your prayer space? In your chart from *Chapter 1* you identified fragrances you liked and how they are dispersed. Look now at how you would like to use them.

Fragrances come to us from all levels: under foot, near our bodies when we brush them with our legs or hands, or surrounding us in the air from aromatic plantings on trellises. Fragrances are also seasonal: crushed leaves when walking in the autumn, lilacs in late spring or an herb garden on a hot summer afternoon.

If you like incense or other "burnt offerings," be sure to identify them in your notes. A trail of smoke from incense or fire offers a visual stimulus as well. In many cultures the trail of smoke is associated with rising prayers and transitions.

Touch

The textures of plants may be part of what leads you to prayer. A pot of woolly Lamb's Ear (*Stachys byzantine* 'Silky Fleece') next to your bench could help alleviate tension when you stroke its thick fuzzy leaves. Maybe the feathery touch of dill, and its resulting aroma as your hand brushes against it, will stimulate memories of making pickles with your grandmother. What would the touch of the soft bark of a beech tree (*Fagus spp.*) bring to mind?

I remember being delightfully surprised one late fall day by my emotions when touching the smooth silvery-green bark of a Curly Willow (*Salix matsudana*). It was soft and had been warmed from the sun and had thousands of distinct petioles forming little yellow-green diamonds all along its stems. As I stood there in awe, letting the tears wash over me, a story about St. Francis of Assisi came to mind. While he was walking down a farm lane one early winter day, Francis was deeply frustrated about his inability to reach the souls of many townspeople. As he approached a leafless apple tree he raised his arm, grabbed a barren limb and shouted at it "Teach me of God!" and as the miracle was recorded, the tree immediately burst into bloom.

We are touched by touching God. How will you bring this sense to life? Is touching part of what draws you to prayer?

Your notes from this chapter have helped you understand how your senses affect your prayer space. The next chapter will help you incorporate what you have identified with other visual influences of design.

Chapter 7

BASIC BUILDING BLOCKS OF DESIGN

"The motivation for creating the garden is more than a search for something to please the eye."[15]

[15]Martin Mosko, *Landscape as Spirit: Creating a Contemplative Garden*, p. 4.

In landscape architecture there are very specific design elements used to create beautiful and amazing outdoor spaces. Several semesters at notable universities are devoted to the topic, as are innumerable books.

Note the first word of this chapter's heading – *basic*. This is the approach that we will take in fostering the design of your small garden space. One of the best workbooks I have found, and often recommend to the beginner, for planning a home landscaping is *Designing Your Gardens and Landscapes; 12 Simple Steps for Successful Planning* by Janet Macunovich.

In this chapter, I will give simple explanations and examples for each of the design elements. Included at the end of this section is a sample worksheet I use in my gardening programs. Recreate it and fill it in to help you refine the plans for your own prayer space. You may, like some of the participants in my classes, be surprised by the emotional influence certain elements have. Once you have filled in the spaces of your form with your notes, add it to your binder.

Simplified Design Elements

Mass, Form and Shape

These elements are very interrelated. Mass is the amount of area, and form or shape is the geometric configuration the mass portrays. Let's take, for example, two kinds of spruce trees; a Cranston Spruce (*Picea abies cranstonii*) can grow to fifty feet high and thirty feet wide, whereas a Dwarf Alberta Spruce (*Picea glauca conica*) usually only grows to eight feet high and about three to four feet wide. Now both of these spruce trees have the same distinct form, being a triangular shape, yet the mass of the Cranston is significantly greater than the mass of the Dwarf Alberta Spruce.

An additional consideration of form and shape is with flowers. This applies to how the flowers are held on the stem and their overall appearance. Consider the mounded form of both the Annabelle Hydrangea (*Hydrangea arborescens* 'Annabelle') and Fireworks Goldenrod (*Solidago rugosa* 'Fireworks'). With the hydrangea the form of the flower is a ball or globe shape, and the goldenrod flowers create a lance or linear shape. Also note that the round mass of the hydrangea bloom is greater than the mass of the linear goldenrod bloom.

Line

This directs the mind, the eye and the direction you will move. It includes how a path is laid out, how your eye follows the layering of plants and how calm or stimulating a space may feel. Spaces with curved lines have a softer shape and are more calming than those that have straight lines and angles and are more stimulating. The way your beds are laid out includes both the line and shape.

A *focal point* is defined as where your eye will go first and rest for a moment. Often times the line of a garden will create a focal point or lead you to one.

Texture and Contrast

Texture is relative and comparative to another surface. Ornamental grasses are considered finer in texture when compared to broader leaf plants like oak trees (*Quercus spp.*) or hostas, but are considered coarser in texture when contrasted with the herb dill (*Anethum graveolens*).

Contrast is similar to texture in that it is the association of two dissimilar objects and can also refer to form, line or color (i.e. round or linear, coarse or fine, curved or straight, saturated or pastel).

A note about texture: the viewing gradient of texture (that is the layering of plants in a vertical interest) from fine to coarse will visually reduce an area and make things appear closer.

To expand the visual appearance of a small area, do the opposite and move from course to medium to fine textures. To do this, mentally break up a small space into thirds. Place the most coarsely-textured materials closest to you in the first third of the area. In the remaining area, place the medium-textured plants or elements in the middle and then the finer-textured plants behind them, the farthest from where you will view them. You will want to use a bit more finely-textured elements than medium-textured ones in this back part of your garden.

Color

Color is a supporting element to the other building blocks. This aspect of design can be understood by looking at a black and white photo of a well-designed garden. The forms, lines and textures present a sense of balance and unity.

If you look at the same picture in color, its deeper beauty is revealed by the way color enhances the boldness of an element. Remember from the previous chapter that color elicits emotions. So, if we take for example the line and texture of a large-leaved hosta, the feel of a garden will change with the color of its leaf – silver-blue, kelly-green or bright chartreuse – even with the hostas being of similar size and shape.

Repetition

Repetition is the reoccurrence of an element throughout the garden. It can be the color of a flower that is also seen on a chair or globe or several of the same plants throughout the garden. Even the bricks used on a building can be repeated in edging or paths and will help unify the space. Everything seems to be more cohesive when the thread of repetition is woven into a garden.

Composition

Composition is the principle of bringing the preceding elements into harmony by using scale, balance, rhythm, emphasis and simplicity.

Scale is relative to size using the average height of a person as the reference point. Something is out of scale when the transition of elements is too abrupt and the object appears too small or too big in its surroundings. A negative example of scale would be an arbor that has a fourteen-foot high arch and only a four-foot width. Its height looks very disproportionate to its width – like a shoebox on end – even when placed near tall trees.

Balance has to do with visual weight and incorporates some of the concepts of scale. We understand what it means to balance physical weights on a bar with a fulcrum underneath; balance can be obtained with multiple smaller objects at one end counterbalancing one larger object. This is the same principle only visually. An example here would be balancing out a tall tree with a wide flower bed nearby.

Nature is asymmetrical and informal, so creating balance has a lot to do with composing and arranging objects in a similar way. It is delightful to watch how people will intuitively seek to create balance in a garden and not know why one arrangement is more pleasing than another. The balance comes from the visual weight of objects seeming to be equal.

Rhythm is similar to repetition in that it adds a sense of unity and cohesiveness to a space. It is the predictability in the repeating of elements. Imagine the rhythm in a long straight path where every eight feet there grows a bright yellow clump of Hakone grass (*Hakonechloa macra* 'Aureola').

Emphasis is also known as the focal point in landscape architecture. You can also consider the intent of your sacred garden as the emphasis or focus of your garden.

Simplicity is achieved by limiting the variety and kinds of elements, such as plants and materials, used in the design of your prayer space. Remember how you have been refining your ideas in each chapter? You have been simplifying your design.

This is a lot of information to process, so take small bites and use the worksheet to help you along. Much of what you will use in designing your small retreat space will feel intuitive. The difference is that now you have the words that coincide with what you already knew.

Design Elements Worksheet

Element	Emotional Connection	Your Notes
Form		
Triangle	Sharp, tense, strong	
Square	Rigid, stable, fixed	
Rectangle	Stable, directed, purposeful	
Circle	Quiet, softness, unbroken, perfect	
Free Form	Casual, imperfect, loose	
Line		
Straight	Formal, firm, stationary	
Angled, squared	Stress, tension, excitement	
Curved	Relaxed, gentleness, flowing	
Texture		
Coarse	Informal, bold, will maintain quality at a distance and appear closer	
Fine (Small garden, 2/3 fine to 1/3 coarse)	Restraint, quietness, refinement; will lose its quality at a distance and appear smoother	
Plant Shape		
Spiked/Vertical	Energy, persistence	
Round/Mound	Serene, cheerful	
Horizontal/ Prostrate	Grounded, openness	
Conical/Pyramidal	Firmness, stability, secure	
Vase/Flaring	Transition, excitement	
Climbing	Movement, reaching, expansiveness	
Weeping	Quietness, calming, softness	
Irregular	Playful, open	

Chapter 8

HARDSCAPE

"The first purpose of a garden is to give happiness and repose of mind."[16]

The hardscape is the nonplant material in your garden. It includes such things as rocks, walkway materials, seating, containers, trellises or obelisks, sacramental objects or art, and buildings or structures. You have already identified what

[16]Hugh Johnson, *Principles of Gardening*, p.2.

hardscape features and other elements you want in your garden and have been clipping pictures of each of them, creating a wish list of sorts. Here is how to narrow down your choices and get a better understanding of your personal style.

Remember those pockets you filled with magazine clippings? Go back to them, one at a time, and look at each collection by topic. Lay all the clippings for that topic on a table and look them over. Now comes the time to narrow them down. This is easy if you're the rare person who only has a half-dozen or so pictures.

Looking at what you have laid out, try to find the theme in all of them. Some of the images will seem not to match what you had defined in *Chapter 1*. Decide if your analysis from the chart you created earlier is weak or if your images are "want to haves" but do not necessarily fit in with your spiritual needs. Ultimately, you will want to narrow down the number of images to only a few for each topic.

Take your time to think about what it is you have defined as an essential element. Of all the images in front of you, discard your least favorite one. Of those that are remaining, discard again until you have only three or four left. A very clear picture of what you like for your prayer space will emerge from this process.

Take those remaining pictures and glue them to a piece of paper, add any comments or notes and add this sheet to your notebook. Continue to do so for each of your essential elements.

You will want to consider your budget. Of the elements

you have selected, which ones are top in priority for you? Rate them at the top of the pages on which you have glued the illustrations.

Which of these elements can you acquire now, even though they may be third or fourth on your list of essentials? Consider a short-term solution for an expensive item until it can be purchased. Can you get by with a green plastic chair and table for a few summers until you can afford the curved willow cane seats and ottoman from the mail order catalog? Maybe you like the looks of a wrought iron obelisk. Can you paint a wooden one black or cobalt blue for the time being?

If you are creating a public space you are probably working within a strict budget. Your desires for the prayer space may include a fountain or sculpture, granite benches and a nice paved walkway. If the fountain or sculpture you've selected works best but is over what was allocated for it, consider adjusting down other items. Can slat benches be used while you fundraise for the granite ones? Can a limestone gravel walkway suffice until pavers can be bought?

Gardens grow—and not only the plants in them. Immediate gratification is a rare event with gardens or the soul. So take the time to decide for yourself what is most necessary for your contemplative space. Your garden of visible prayer is coming to life.

Chapter 9

PLANT SELECTION

"Flowers are fleeting but texture is timeless."[17]

Plant selection is one the more rewarding occupations of garden design. Getting just that right plant in the right place, both visually and physiologically, is fulfilling. In a garden space that is small, it is matter of preference whether to select plants before or after you have your garden's design drawn.

When selecting plants before drawing out your design, you will start by creating your plant vocabulary for the

[17]Margaret Realy, *Lecture Series: Easiest Plants to Grow.*

site. This is a list of the plants that you like and will grow in that location. Not all of the plants listed will be used, but you will have a set of options when you need them.

If you draw your design first, laying in paths, seating and other hardscape elements, you will know that you want a shrub here or ornamental grasses there. It is after you have done this simple drawing that you will go to your garden books and select specific plants. The next chapter will guide you in creating your drawings.

Whatever is easiest for you to do – selecting the plants first or drawing the space – do it. Whatever allows your creative nature to flow, follow it. I have used either method for creating prayer gardens and found them both to be successful.

If your sacred space will use container plantings instead of an installed garden, your task will be much simpler. Only a portion of what follows will apply. Not only do you have a smaller plant vocabulary to create, you can change it from year to year.

For an installed garden you will need to know what Hardiness Zone you live in. This will tell you what plants will survive in your area (zone). There are both cold and heat considerations for hardiness. A hardiness zone tells you that a plant grown in that area can endure a fifty percent kill off of its root because of temperature and still survive. There is an example of a cold Hardiness Zone map of the continental United States in *Chapter 13*. You might also check gardening resources in your area, such as your county extension office or a reputable nursery to get accurate information.

Plant Vocabulary

You will now use the features in the Site Assessment you made in *Chapter 5*. What had you concluded about shade and sunlight, and what areas are involved? What are the characteristics of the soil? Is the site dry because it is on a slope or in full sunlight? Will plants have to contend with others with stronger or established root systems?

To create a chart of your plant vocabulary, make a table with columns and write the features of the site at the top. The first column will be for the name of the plant. Each succeeding column should be labeled with the feature of the site: full sun, dense shade, dry, rocky, etc. Start your plant vocabulary by listing existing plants at your proposed prayer garden site. Not only will this help you familiarize yourself with using the table you have just created but it will assist you in looking up plants on the Internet or in other reference tools.

As you select a plant, write its name and include the color and season of bloom if it flowers and put a check mark in the column that matches its characteristic.

You may want to include columns that designate the texture of a plant, its mature size (height and width) and form. Reference materials and labels that come with the plant will tell you the plant's mature size. The Design Elements Worksheet created in *Chapter 8* helps you to think about what forms, line, textures and shapes work best for your spiritual space.

One of my key phrases, reiterated often in my gardening programs, is to select the right plant for the right place. You may love the yellow variegated color and texture of Hakone Grass (*Hakonechloa macra* 'Aureola') but it will be of no use planted in the western sun of a sandy site. It needs high shade and moist, well-drained soil.

I often found myself clipping pictures of plants as I collected ideas for a garden. If you too have collected pictures of flowers and shrubs, write those names of plants next in your table and record their characteristics.

A side note here: many people also include the "meaning" of plants in their selection process. This feature is similar to the influential energy of colors. For example, to some people the birch tree (*Betula papyrifera*) is thought to cultivate spiritual wisdom; the carnation (*Dianthus spp.*), whose name literally means *Flower of God*, represents Mary and the incarnation of Jesus.

Keep in mind that the meanings of a plant are culturally diverse and have different meanings in different religions: a person of Irish decent may have a very different association for poppies than someone from the Middle

East. Definitely do some research into the meanings or historical allusions associated with certain plants if that brings you closer to your sacred place. There are many resources available to help in the search.

As you progress through your design and selection process, keep it simple. I often teach new gardeners my Rule of Three:

- Three heights
- Three textures
- Three colors
- Three seasons

This simple rule applies both to containers and installed gardens and will help you avoid being overwhelmed by the sheer number of available options. And everything does not need to flower. Not until recently were flowers considered the mainstay of a garden. Before that it was the form and texture of plants.

Planting Options

You have established the intent of your garden and what its style will be. Consider some of the following in your plant selection process:

Native Plants

When an area is located in a naturalistic setting, one option is to enhance your new garden by using native plants. For those of you who are ecology-minded, this will enhance your connectedness to the system of nature already in place. The other benefit of working with native plants is that they will require less support from you because they are already matched to the environment; there is reduced need for fertilization, disease control and watering. Native plants will also encourage local birds and butterflies into your prayer space.

Reduced Pollen

If you have allergies or an aversion to insects, look for information on allergy-free gardening. In creating a garden for the visually impaired, use this information to draw bees

and other pollinators away from areas where people might be in danger of being stung if they touched certain plants.

Night Gardens or Moon Gardens

It is a challenge but very fulfilling to design a garden like this, especially if you will be using your space after sunset. Look for flowers that are very light pastels or all white, that bloom in the evening (check local resources for your zone), and mix in leaves that are very light and/or variegated. It can take your breath away to see a garden glowing in the moonlight.

Potager*

This is a very popular concept that has come into its own in the United States but has existed in Europe for centuries. Sometimes thought of as an edible landscape, this kind of garden uses essential design elements when incorporating fruits and vegetables into the landscape. There are many associations with spirituality in a potager: the idea of being nourished, a focus on family, bearing fruit, to mention a few.

Container Gardening

Planters offer a great deal of diversity. You can use containers exclusively on porches and decks or incorporate them into your garden space. You can use planters to resolve problems when soils are unworkable from compaction, contamination or tree roots.

*(pronounced poot•ú•jee)

Container gardens are helpful in other ways, too. Once I had to design a garden in a section of soil that was next to a sidewalk leading to a main entrance. Heavy equipment had compacted the soil and it had been contaminated with oils and cleaning solvents. This rather large area would not support any plants and I had to find a solution to the eyesore. Digging out and replacing the soil was too costly, not to mention the problem of the existence of utility lines and trees. To solve this problem I picked up and recycled oblong cattle watering troughs, drilled them for better drainage, set them in place, filled them with a shallow layer of gravel, half filled them with composted material and then added eight inches of potting mix. I then enclosed the troughs with a decorative wood facing and planted a variety of annuals and grasses in them. So container gardens can be large-scale as this one was.

The next chapter will expand on the technique of creating container gardens.

Don't stop looking for plant combinations once your garden is created. Continue expanding your plant vocabulary for diversifying the plants in your sacred space as the years go by. You may find you want to add something more after you have used your area a while or add something new to another part of your property.

Chapter 10

CONTAINER GARDENS

"A minute shift in focus, of attention, will unveil a feast of the sacred within our every day."[18]

Making a container garden is simpler than most people think. By following a few rules you can create a wonderful addition to your prayer space. A side note here: you can also make an edible container garden using the same instructions.[19]

---

[18]Grimsley & Young, *Contemplative by Design*, p.9.
[19]McGee & Stuckey, *Bountiful Container* is a great resource.

The containers you will use are usually chosen because of aesthetics, but let's also consider their function. There are some things to keep in mind about the containers themselves. Remember to consider the weight of a container, especially if you need to move it for winter storage. Also consider the color of your container. When exposed to direct sunlight, a black or dark-colored exterior will get hot and increase the soil temperature inside the container, damaging the roots of plants that are not heat-tolerant. To help prevent overheating you can choose a container of a lighter color. You can also put something in front of the container to shade the bottom during the hottest part of the day. Another option is to insulate the inside walls of the container before filling it using styrofoam sheets cut into vertical strips.

The following chart will help you decide what will work best for your purpose.

Container Characteristics

Container Type	Moisture Retention	Weight	U.V. Resistant	Winter
Clay/ Ceramics	Average	Moderately heavy, smaller pieces moveable	Yes	Not winter proof
Concrete	Average to high, adequate drainage a must	Heavy, stationary	Yes	Usually winter proof
Fiber	Dries quickly	Light, most will split easily when moved	No	Not winter proof
Fiberglass	Very high	Light, smaller pieces moveable	Usually not, check supplier	Not winter proof
Metal	Very high	Light to moderately heavy, usually moveable	Yes	Winter proof
Moss	Very low, use a reservoir inside container	Moderate, moveable depends on size	Depends on material used	Winter proof
Plastic	Very high	Very light, even for large pots	Usually not, check supplier	Not winter proof
Terra cotta	Average	A bit heavy, larger pieces are stationary	Yes	Not winter proof
Wood	Average	Moderately heavy usually moveable	Somewhat	Not winter proof

When filling your container use only potting mix not soil. Soil will compact and inhibit root development. Do not use filler in the bottom of larger pots. Research has shown that plants whose roots have grown into that air space are weaker and are prone to disease. If you do have a large container that you cannot afford to fill with potting mix, use a smaller container that will fit inside. Place an upended pot in the bottom of your large pot for your smaller pot to rest on or use bricks stacked to the optimum height. A smaller container inside a larger one is also a good solution for preventing the soil from overheating if you use a container that is dark in color.

With excessively large containers, as was the case with the recycled watering troughs mentioned in the previous chapter, add potting mix on top to a depth of eight inches. This is the depth of the root system of most annual plants. Fill the remaining lower portion with composted material, which is lighter than soils.

If you are going to place your container on a wood deck, or, for that matter, any hard surface, be sure to raise the container at least a half inch off the surface. This will ensure the container gets proper drainage and also prevents damage or stains on the surface where you placed it. You can use any number of items to support the container, from coordinated footings that match the pot to recycled bricks.

When you design your container think about how it will

be viewed when you are in your space. Will you see it from all sides? Do you intend to place it against a wall or in a corner? Will you use a series of containers to divide a space or create shade?

A container that is seen from all sides should have a circular design with the focal point at the center. A container placed against a wall or in a corner will look best in a half-moon design with the focal point near the back. If you intend to add an item to your container, such as a globe or statue, place it slightly forward from the center and elevated: as the plants grow you do not want them to hide the main attraction. When you line up large containers in a row, such as a divider for your prayer space, consider which side will be facing the sun. The taller plants in the middle of your container will shade the plants on the opposite side. Unless you plan on rotating your containers weekly, use shade-tolerant plants on that side.

Keep the design of your container simple by using the Rule of Three as mentioned in *Chapter 9*. You will want three colors, three textures and three heights, one of which should be trailing so the plant will fall over the edge of the container.

You should decide how many plants to buy based on the plants' overall size at maturity. Read the plant tags to know how big the plants will get, and then purchase about a third more. The reasoning here is that you will want to create a lush container and container grown plants rarely achieve their full growth. So if it would take four plants to fill a garden space of the same size, add one more for your container and buy five.

Try to create a planting plan using odd numbers; i.e. one in the middle, three at the next ring, and three to five on the outer edge, depending on the size of your container. Odd number plants are more pleasing and create less visual tension.

By applying what you have learned about containers throughout this book, you will create a beautiful addition for your sacred space.

Chapter 11

DRAWING IT OUT

"[The garden] doesn't have to be elaborate; it just has to be soulful."[20]

You have collected all the information on what leads you to an outdoor place of solace. You have the pictures of where your space will be located, your worksheets, the illustrations of the hardscape items, and a list of plant materials. All of which you have narrowed down to a select few and can now start to pull them all together.

[20]Nancy Endres, *The Healing Garden*, Midwest Living, p. 110.

For those of you placing your retreat area on a deck or porch, your drawing efforts will be minimal. Be sure to use the plan view for creating your containers.

Landscape architecture is designed with two drawing views: elevation view and plan view. The elevation drawing is oriented from eye level looking directly at the area to give you a sense of scale, line and form. You draw the house with the shrub under the window and the rock in front of the shrub. The plan drawing is looking down on the area as if from a bird's-eye or aerial view. This eventually becomes your planting plan.

Creating a Worksheet

This section will help you create worksheets to be used for drawing your designs. How to draw each view, step-by-step, will come a little later in the chapter.

For creating the elevation view you should already have a picture looking directly at your chair and two more pictures from each side, as if you were standing next to and behind the chair. This is unlike the plan view where you will consider all of the area at once.

If you can, have the photos of your area enlarged to an 8½ x 11 image. Be sure to crop the pictures first to include a fairly narrow view of the space – you really don't need a lot of lawn or the whole driveway in the picture. Lay a piece of tracing paper over your enlarged picture, and trace a general outline of the area, your chair, and any significant features such as existing trees or arbors. Make several tracings or copies of the general outline for each picture. These will be your worksheets for the elevated view.

Drawing the plan view is usually done after the elevation view sketches have been selected. To create the worksheet for your plan view you will need to measure off the width and depth of the space and draw in existing elements and their sizes. It is important to be accurate. Usually these drawings are done on a quarter-inch-square graph paper, but to make it easy to draw to scale, you could use a 1:1 scale where one foot equals one inch. Start by drawing in the trees. Draw the size of the trunk and, with a light, dotted line, draw the area of ground covered by the tree's canopy. Make several copies of your plan view as you did for the elevation views.

Expect to make several drawings of each view as you play with your ideas. All these drawings will help you decide what you like or don't like.

Elevation View

Start drawing by placing your hardscape images in front of you on your work area, and then get the directly-in-front-of-chair view of your elevated worksheet drawing. When you draw, try to keep the scale of the objects in mind as best you can. Do not worry about drawing things perfectly. Remember most of us are not artists and, besides, nobody else needs to see your drawings.

Your tracing already has the chair in it, so draw the seating you want for your garden over it, and then add

the larger foundation items such as the arbor, trees, water feature or gates.

Once you have the foundation (also known as background) in place you can begin to layer the mid-sized items that are two to three feet high, like bird baths, boulders and so on, and finish with the smaller hardscape details. Remember to draw in a path if you have one. Do the same with the other two sides of your elevated view. You will find that you are drawing one thing on top of another; that is exactly the right thing to be doing. Try using colored pencils for each layer and erase background lines as you go.

Repeat this process with your plant material, using the size of a nearly mature plant as your guide. For references, set the pictures you have collected on your work area along with the plant list chart. Starting with the foundation plants, draw those that are taller at the back of the view, then draw in the mid-sized plants and lastly the smaller plants which will be in front. Use capital letters to identify which plants will go where; i.e. daylilies are marked with an "A", groundcover with a "B," and so on. Write the corresponding letter next to the plant's name on the list.

Unless you're very good at drawing you should have a lot of messy-looking layouts. Look over each set of your elevation views. As before, pull your least favorite layout from the lineup and discard it. Continue this process, redrawing if necessary, until you are satisfied with one layout for each elevated view.

Plan View

The plan view drawings take less time. You already have the correct dimensions, existing structures and plants drawn. You will transfer the images from the elevated view drawings to your plan view. Working with the elevated views you decided to keep, draw the seating, path, water feature and/or other hardscape elements on to your plan view.

As before, try to keep your elements to scale. There are special rulers and templates available, if you know how to calculate and use them. If not, try this procedure:

1. Let's say your retreat area is 8 x 6 feet, convert that to 8 x 6 inches on your paper. (This is a 1 foot = 1 inch scale, or 1:1.)

2. Draw in any existing structures using the 1:1 scale.

3. You may know the size of your chair or bench or table, draw that in at the 1:1 scale.

4. Do this again for your walkway or arbor.

That's all there is to it. You now have an idea of how the measurements of feet to inches will scale down items as you draw them in your plan. Keep this in mind as you add in plants.

With many plants, especially annuals and perennials, overlapping them a little or planting them in a group will create a different appearance (mass and form) as the plants mature. You see this in many gardens where there are multiple annual plants of the same species put together to create a mound of color. If the selected plant is to stand alone, as in a collection of Karl Foerster's Grass (*Calamagrostis x acutiflora* 'Karl Foerster'), each plant repeats the shape of the others and is enhanced by the space between them.

Again, make as many drawings as you can. Follow the same procedure as before: pull out and discard your least favorite layouts until you have your final plan view.

You will use this final drawing to make your shopping list for materials and plants. It is also your planting plan as you begin installation.

Chapter 12

PREPARATION AND INSTALLATION

We come to know God through the palms of our hands.[21]

The anticipation of getting to this point has accompanied you through each step in your discernment of your outdoor prayer space. Finally, and with a full appreciation of this process and a careful assembling of your notes, the birth of your sacred space is about to take place.

[21] Margaret Realy, *Lecture Series: Creating a Memorial or Prayer Garden.*

Preparation of the site for creating a new garden space is more intensive than adapting an existing garden or part of a structure. In preparing your site, try to think about the fact that you are in a sense creating "holy ground." Offer up your efforts to acknowledge spiritual movement and to foster a sense of sanctuary. This is not just another pretty space.

Later in the process you can include children, family or friends in creating your retreat area if you need assistance or want them to share in the installation process. But at first, begin this process quietly, alone with your spirit.

The last item to be brought into your space is the object that you had previously selected as the meditative or prayer focus. When you introduce this item into your garden, such as an incense burner, statue or specific plant, it will complete the development process.

Non-Garden Adaptation

With an area that is part of an existing porch or deck, there are a few things you can do to help you mentally see the area as sanctuary. Begin by taking all movable objects from the space, even those items that you will be using. Then sweep. Yes, I know it seems obvious that you'll want to get rid of the dirt, but there is more to this than removing debris. Imagine that you are spiritually sweeping away the abrasiveness and hardness, the darkness and struggles, the disruption and chaos of daily living.

Having swept out the debris, cleanse the area. Not necessarily with bucket and mop (though maybe the porch

could use a good wash), but in the spirit of a ritual cleansing. This can be as simple as sweeping a handful of purifying herbs over the area or as elaborate as having a priest come to bless it. You could touch the corners of the area with special oils or water, burn incense or say prayers. Whatever you decide will be perfect for you. But don't skip this step even though it may feel awkward.

When you have completed this cleansing, the first item to bring into your area will be the seating, or if this is your selected prayer item, an alternate chair or bench. Following your drawings, place your hardscape items where they belong. Use your seat/chair/bench as a reference point so you can check the view to be certain you like the results.

Now, if you had designed for them, install your plants at the edge of your area or put your container of plants in place. You may find, as all designers do, that slight adjustments may be needed once you sit and look around at your work.

Once you are satisfied with your efforts, quietly and prayerfully, bring the object that represents your meditative focus into your area.

In-Ground Garden Installation

The process you use is the same as for any landscape installation.

As I mentioned before, you begin mentally sanctifying the area by removing debris by raking, pulling weeds or doing some sort of personal preparatory activity. As you work imagine you are removing from your area those disruptions that press down on your peace and centeredness.

Then choose a means to signify cleansing the area. As previously mentioned, you can do so with herbs, special oils or water. You also could make a small twig fire while meditating, or as a Catholic friend once did, hang a rosary on a low branch and prayerfully ask for blessings.

With your drawing in hand, place the seating where you intend it to be or use something similar on which to sit as you work. Mark off your garden outline, paths and/or beds. One of my favorite ways is the old garden hose trick: lay the hose on the ground in the outline you desire and mark the outline using spray paint, bone meal or, my choice, handfuls of soil.

If you are creating a new or unusually shaped flower bed, narrowly trench out your outline using a spade and remove unwanted plants or sod. Any soil amendments should be added at this time; compost is always a good thing.

The next phase is even more labor intensive. At this point you install your hardscape and any large ornamental trees. This will include everything from walkways and edgings to permanent structures. When laying pavers or using cement for posts, check appropriate references for proper installation. If you intend to lay a ground cloth as a weed barrier, do so after the main features are in place.

As you work out the bones of your space, be sure to sit back at times and observe your progress. Do this from the location of your preferred garden seat. This will allow you to look at your drawings and check the view to ensure that all is going according to your plan. As I already mentioned, all designs are tweaked along the way. So remain confident in the drawings you have developed knowing that minor site-related adjustments will occur.

Before you begin the last phase in installation, take a few minutes to look around your small space from inside the retreat area. Are you feeling content with what you have done? Have you relocated the garbage cans or dug out that shrub you really didn't want? Are all but your designated object in place as you planned? Is the water feature or gate or lighting working properly? Take the time to breathe; this is your place of solace. It is an interior view of your personal sacred journey on many levels.

As you prepare for planting remember you will work from the tallest to the shortest, from the farthest to the nearest, or if circular, from the outside toward the center seating area.

On the afternoon before you intend to put plants in or move them, thoroughly water them. This will help reduce the stress of transplanting. For more information about transplanting, see *Chapter 13: From Pot to Garden*. If it hasn't rained in a several days and your soil seems dry when you dig about four inches down below the surface, water the area you will be planting about forty-eight hours beforehand. Evenly moist but not wet soil is easier to work and, again, reduces the stress to plants. If you think that the afternoon sun will be too intense for your new plants, put them in later in the day. There is no rule saying that you have to garden in the mornings.

When the area is properly moist, it is time to get planting. Leaving your plants in their pots, place them as indicated by your plan drawing in your garden area. You will often find it necessary to adjust the potted plants

after you get them set in place – maybe one is too close to the fence or another grouping is too tight. Keep in mind the mature size of your plant as you work. Be sure to rotate the plants so the nicest side faces the viewer, or that the shape of the branches forms a pleasing visual line that you can see from where you will be sitting.

If you are working through ground cloth, cut an "X" about twenty-five percent larger than the hole you will dig where you intend to plant. Pull back the flaps, dig, plant, and lay the flaps back in place. Be sure to tuck the flaps so they don't show against the trunk or stems.

To prevent damage to the smaller plants designated in your plan, wait until after the larger ones are in the ground to place them.

Oftentimes smaller plants are purchased in trays or flats of trays. Individual plants in these types of carriers are sometimes called plugs. Don't pop them out of their trays just yet. Set the entire pack in the area where those plugs will be planted. Once you are satisfied with their arrangement, put them in the ground too, spaced according to their mature size.

If you intended to use mulch you can work from one side to the other or from back to front. Here is a trick to help with spreading it: remember all those pots from the plants you just put in? After knocking out the excess dirt from inside the pot, turn it upside down, and as you place it on the ground, tuck your plant inside. After you have spread the mulch, pull off the pot and your precious little plant is nice and clean. In an area where you have several

plugs, use smaller pots or plastic cups. My method is to cover about twelve to fifteen plants and shift to the next set of plants once the initial area is mulched. This seems to go a lot faster than trying to cover all the little ones beforehand.

Your planting may look barer than you had anticipated, but don't be dismayed. Give it time. Remember that gardens grow into their surroundings, as do our souls.

You have arranged, planted, watered and mulched. It is now time to place your designated object of prayer focus and bring your project to completion. In a memorial garden, this object could be the dedication plaque. In a private garden it could be the birdbath, a rock or the seating. Whatever it is, now is the time to place it reverently in your personal sacred space.

Enjoy your garden. Use it. As you learn to find solace in your space, remember that you can come to a garden but not to garden. There will be times for tending your garden, both spiritually and physically.

God's choicest blessings as all things grow.

Chapter 13

ET CETERA, ET CETERA, ET CETERA

We learn more in the doing than in the being told.[22]

[22]From my grandmother Margaret (Angott) Warrilow who repeatedly brought this to my attention during distracted adolescent years.

This chapter is a collection of information that does not fit well into the flow of the book. For additional information on gardening techniques, look into any number of resources on the subject. There are a few listed in the *Annotated Bibliography.*

Reading a Plant Tag

Most retailers sell plants with tags from the supplier/grower giving you information about the potted plant.

Besides the botanical name and general description of the appearance of the plant, specifics are provided and should include Hardiness Zone and may include bloom period, divisional needs, or pruning information. How to Grow information will include light requirements, water needs, height range and average spread. The last bit of information – width – will indicate how far apart to place plants. You can use this information as you create your Plant Vocabulary Chart mentioned in *Chapter 9, Plant Selection.*

Calculating Plants

To know how many plants you will need to purchase for your garden, you first need to figure out how many square feet there are. If your area is closer to a square or a rectangle, measure the length and the width of your space. Multiply the two together. If your area is similar to a circle, stretch a tape measurer across the widest part of the circle, and then multiply it by 3.14.

Once you know how many square feet you will be planting, you can figure how many plants will fit in that area. The spacing information is on the plant's tag and tells you how far apart to plant each one. By using the following chart, you will know how many plants to buy for each square foot you've calculated.

This may seem excessive for a small garden when you are able to determine that you only need three or four plants. But for those of you working on larger, new or public prayer gardens the spacing multiplier is invaluable.

Spacing Multiplier

This is a very simple procedure: take the square feet that you calculated and multiply it by the number in the second column, based on the spacing information for the plant in the first column.

Spacing between plants	Spacing Multiplier; how many plants needed per sq. ft.
4"	9
5"	5.76
6"	4
7"	2.94
8"	2.25
9"	1.78
10"	1.45
11"	1.19
12"	1
15"	0.64
18"	0.44
24"	0.25
30"	0.16
36"	0.11

From Pot to Garden

The first rule for all potted plants is that the level of soil around the plant in the garden should be the same level as the soil in the pot. Planting something too high will expose its roots to air. It will also dry out the root ball more quickly. Plant too deeply and the stem, crown (the base of a perennial plant where the stems emerge), or trunk of the plant can rot from lack of air and sunlight.

The process for transplanting starts the night before with watering the pots. Plants take up and hold the largest percentage of water during the night. Your plants will be better able to withstand root disturbances that inhibit water intake during the day when the cells of the plant are turgid – already full of water. If you plan on planting them later in the day after the harshest sun has passed, then set the watered pots in a shaded location until then.

There is only a slight difference between planting herbaceous plants like perennials and annuals and planting hardwoods such as trees and shrubs. Research has shown that larger hardwoods need to have the same soil that was dug out reused to backfill the hole and should not have the soil altered by amendments. Adding *mychorrizae* inoculants to enhance root development is fine.

The reason for not enhancing the soil is because the root system is less likely to expand beyond the amended soil into harder, less nutrient-rich soil. This causes the roots to form a circular mass that will eventually fill the space – eliminating the necessary proportion of soil to root mass and creating a potential for girdling – the roots literally strangle themselves and ultimately kill the plant. It is always best to select the right plant for the site with its existing soil condition.

These are the steps for planting either herbaceous or hardwood plants:

1. Dig the hole twice as wide and 1½ times as deep as the container or root ball.

2. For herbaceous plants, amend the soil with compost.

3. Use enough soil to raise the bottom of the hole to the same height as the container or root ball. Remember, you want the soil level of the container or pot to be the same height as the top of the hole when you're finished.

4. Add *mychorrizae* inoculants to the bottom of hole to enhance root development and mix with some of the removed soil.

5. Remove plants from their container or root ball wrap (yes, remove the burlap and wire it was shipped in), and carefully loosen their roots. If the roots are severely entangled, or root-bound, you may need to make three or four minor cuts into the sides of the root mass near the bottom in order to be able to pull them apart.

6. Place the plant in the hole, spreading the roots evenly and adding a little water. Use a liquid transplant fertilizer, organic or commercial, at this point of watering. Again, be sure the plant will be at same soil level.

7. Backfill the hole with soil, making sure you avoid air pockets. Pack it slightly with your hands as you go. Don't compact soil by pressing it down really hard or stomping on it.

8. Build up the soil away from the central stem or crown. This forms a moat around the plant that will help contain the water.

9. Water thoroughly. If you have transplanted a very large tree and the root ball seemed dry, leave the hose to drip water near the trunk for three or four hours to saturate it.

10. For larger trees, stake the trunk to prevent the tree from tipping during the first year while the root system expands. Use three stakes placed about three to four feet away from the trunk and evenly spaced around it. When the stakes are pounded into the ground they need to be at least one half the height of the trunk. Run heavy gauge wire through twelve- to fourteen-inch sections of old hose. Rest the hose against the trunk and secure each end of the wire to your stakes. Do not pull the wires too tight. You want to stabilize the tree, not choke it.

11. Mulch the area up to ridge of the moat. After your plant is established, you can level the moat and cover this area with mulch as well. Herbaceous plants are usually

established in a few weeks. Hardwoods, especially larger trees may take several months.

Transplanting

Transplanting is best done in the spring or, for trees and shrubs, early autumn. If you find that you will be transplanting during the summer, anticipate the need to protect your plants from excessive sunlight, heat and wind until they are established enough to take up the necessary water (about 10-14 days for herbaceous plants).

A method I use involves rigging shade from white pillowcases and sheets picked up at yard sales or resale stores. The white fabric diffuses direct sunlight without creating excessive shade. For taller plants, drive posts into the ground so they will be about a third higher than the plant on the sides where the sun and wind come from. Attach the fabric to the posts with safety pins or garden wire to form a wall. For plants that are very short, place a single layer of white fabric on top before the hottest part of the day, and secure with handfuls of mulch or small rocks. Be sure to pull back the material in late afternoon to allow the plants to breathe during the night and early morning hours.

Planting Under Trees

First you may need to improve the soil. If you do, take care not to harm the tree's roots or trunk. After all, it is the tree you appreciate and want to flourish.

The procedure of improving the soil will take a few years (about two or three) before you can make your final planting. Using containers until that time lets you make use of the space until you can plant your garden permanently around the tree.

Remember that trees are heavy feeders and big drinkers. Even with soil conditioning, your garden under their limbs will need special consideration with regard to planning, plant selection, water and fertilizing.

You can enrich the soil with thoroughly composted organic matter and leaves. The tree already provides the biggest part of the conditioning material needed – the leaves. Gather the leaves and chop them into small pieces using a yard chopper or bagging-style lawn mower. Combine the organic matter and leaves and spread it under the tree at no more than four inches deep per season. Be sure to stay about six to eight inches away from the trunk. Sprinkle with a little compost activator, or use finely-chopped yarrow (*Achillea millefolium*) clippings, and water the area. Keep this area moist (but not waterlogged) until winter.

Mow down any weeds that may take root during the following summer, being careful not to damage any "tree-knees" – the roots exposed on the surface. Pile on the next round of chopped leaves the following autumn.

Repeat this procedure one more time, adding enough compost to create a raised bed eight to ten inches at the outer edge to less than one inch near the trunk. Do not build up compost around the tree trunk. The skirt at the base of the tree, that section at ground level that flares out from the vertical trunk, should be exposed to air movement. Now let the – as I have named them – "earthworks" (microbes, worms and bugs) move in and loosen the composted soil for you. By the third summer you should have a nice, soft, friable soil and it will be possible to plant your shade garden under the boughs of your beautiful tree.

Fertilizing

To insure the health of your plants, always have a soil analysis done before adding a lot of fertilizers or nutrients. A county extension officer or other soil analysis services can help you with this testing. What follows on page 126 is a chart of different types of fertilizers and amendments that you can add to your soil. This information was adapted from the book *Bountiful Container*.[23]

Soil pH (level of acidity) is crucial to nutrient uptake in plants. Most plants prefer a soil pH between 6.0-7.0. If the pH is outside this range, plants cannot absorb the necessary nutrients.

Begin with a basic and complete fertilizer. Your soil analysis will tell you how to add supplements. Remember, using more is usually not better when it comes to fertilizing.

What does N-P-K apply to?

Here is a little ditty that I created and use as a handout for the programs I present. Participants who are not experienced

[23]McGee & Stuckey, *Bountiful Container*, p. 69.

gardeners commented that they found it very helpful in remembering the codes for fertilizers.

<u>N</u> = Nitrogen = <u>N</u>ice Leaves

<u>P</u> = Phosphorous = <u>ph</u>lowers & <u>ph</u>ruit

<u>K</u> = Potassium = that which you <u>K</u>eep covered, or for what is <u>pot</u>ted beneath – the roots.

When you look at the analysis on the package of a fertilizer you will have a better understanding of what each number means in relation to your plants.

Fertilizer & Amendment Chart

Kind	Form	Type	Predominate Nutrients	Additional Nutrients
Bat Guano	Powder, Granule	Organic	Nitrogen, Phosphorus	Macro and micronutrients
Blood meal	Powder	Organic	Nitrogen	
Bone meal	Powder	Organic	Phosphorous	Nitrogen
Bulb food	Powder	Inorganic	Phosphorous	Nitrogen, potassium
Dolomite lime	Powder	Inorganic	Calcium	Magnesium, also raises pH
Fish emulsion	Liquid	Organic	Nitrogen	Phosphorus, potassium
Greensand	Powder Granule	Organic	Potassium	Magnesium, micronutrients
Liquid seaweed	Liquid	Organic	Potassium	Nitrogen, micronutrients, trace elements
Magnesium sulfate	Powder	Inorganic	Sulfur, magnesium	
Mushroom compost	Granule	Organic	Potassium, Nitrogen	Macro and Micronutrients, trace elements
Rock phosphate	Powder	Organic	Phosphorus	Micronutrients Calcium
Super-phosphate	Powder	Inorganic	Phosphorus	Sulfur
Worm castings	Powder, Granule	Organic	Nitrogen	Calcium, micronutrients

U.S.D.A. HARDINESS ZONE MAP
OF THE UNITES STATES

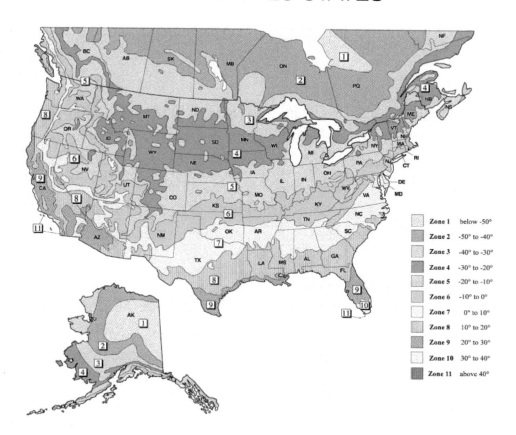

Zone 1	below -50°
Zone 2	-50° to -40°
Zone 3	-40° to -30°
Zone 4	-30° to -20°
Zone 5	-20° to -10°
Zone 6	-10° to 0°
Zone 7	0° to 10°
Zone 8	10° to 20°
Zone 9	20° to 30°
Zone 10	30° to 40°
Zone 11	above 40°

Appendix A

CATHOLIC TRADITIONS
IN PRAYER GARDENS

As Catholics, we have a rich heritage of religious traditions. Most are universal to our faith and some are culturally distinct. All are grounded in our celebrating God's love.

Listed here are some traditions of the Catholic faith that can be converted into an outdoor prayer space.

Stations of the Cross

This type of a prayer garden will include all fourteen Stations of the Cross. Some of the ways to feature them would be with handmade stepping stones, a verse from the Bible stamped or painted on cement, or purchased plaques mounted on posts. You can also plant flowers whose names or shapes evoke the Stations of the Cross.

More often than not the Stations are situated along a path in a single or double row with the Stations facing each other. Another way to arrange the Stations is in a circle with a bench, statue or tree at the center. They also can be placed along a meandering path as I saw at a private residence where rustic handmade mosaics were placed on log posts along a path encircling a pond.

Rosary

This Catholic tradition lends itself well to a garden setting. By keeping in mind the basic order and elements of the rosary – cross, center, six *Pater* beads and fifty-three *Mater* beads – you can be very creative in how you construct your garden.

Like the Stations of the Cross, you can use flowers whose names and form evoke the mysteries of the rosary. You can also use small stones encircling a statue or seating area, or several colored pavers laid in a path.

A parochial school I know of has the most delightful Rosary garden I had ever seen. Several children made colorful cement stepping stones to represent the beads: octagonal steppers for the *Pater* beads, square ones for the *Mater*. A cement cross marked the entrance to the garden and a small statue of Mary surrounded by a little flower bed of yellow Calendula[24] denotes the center of the rosary. The pavers are set in a path that winds between boulders and trees, ending at the other side of the school.

Marian Devotions

Marian gardens are filled with plants named for Mary and Jesus. A statue or image of Mary is always included in the garden. These gardens are usually enclosed in some way. Enclosing the garden comes from a verse in the Bible, Song of Songs 4:12, "You are an enclosed garden, my sister, my bride, an enclosed garden, a fountain sealed."

Saints, Shrines and Devotionals

These gardens are often created with a sense of gratitude to God and the special saint for blessings and answered prayers. These gardens are also places to say prayers for protection, petition or in memory of an event or special favor.

[24]*Calendula officianalis* was called Mary's Gold in honor of the Virgin Mary. In some parts of the world where Calendula didn't grow, the familiar *Tagetes spp.* soon took on the name Marigold for this same reason.

Shrines are usually open to the public as a stopping place to pray, so consider sharing this type of garden space.

There are many saints and holy people who are prayed to in petition and thanksgiving. Following close behind Marian gardens is St. Francis. St. Francis of Assisi is a popular saint in the garden because of his recognition of the creator's hand in all of nature. St. Fiacre is the patron saint of gardeners, especially for gardens that produce food. St. Therese of Lisieux is known for leaving roses in her wake. A book of saints will help you choose a patron if you haven't one already.

Angels

Angels are known to be guardians, messengers and protectors who help us fight against evil. The Archangels are St. Michael, St. Gabriel, St. Raphael and St. Uriel, the last of whom is not mentioned in Holy Scripture.

Angels are one of the most popular images in gardens with any number of garden statuary pieces available on the market.

Labyrinth

When Christians could not make visits to the Holy Land, labyrinths came to be used as substitutes for the Way of the Cross. Christians would walk the labyrinths, often on their knees in penance, meditating on the Passion of Our Lord, as they went.

There is only one way in or out of a labyrinth and only one path to the center, which represents our Lord or heaven. Though directed towards the center, that path is a winding road, just like our lives, full of unforeseen turns and hardship, and this is especially true if that path is traveled on one's knees. Yet, to a person following the way through the labyrinth, the center is always in view. If we stay on the path we will eventually find ourselves where we want to be.

Labyrinths can be simple and constructed easily in grassy areas using plants or stones to earmark the path, or they can be made more elaborate using beautiful granite pavers.

Bible Verses or Themes

As I mentioned earlier in this book, one of my favorite elements in a prayer garden is a Bible verse stamped into cement. The selected verse should hold a special meaning for you to meditate on, much like *lectio divina*. My personal favorite is "Be still and know that I am God."

A Bible theme, on the other hand, is inspired by a story or book in Holy Scripture. A garden created to follow a theme, as in a journey could use a series of paths, or maybe the Garden of Gethsemane with a large boulder as the focal point. You could plant a white garden to represent the light of Christ or the Transfiguration.

Plants of the Bible

There are many resources available to find lists of plants mentioned in the Bible, and plants whose names or forms evoke biblical themes. Check you local library or search the Internet to find this information.

ANNOTATED BIBLIOGRAPHY

Armitage, Allan M. *Armitage's Manual of Annuals, Biennials, and Half-Hardy Perennials.* Portland, OR: Timber Press, Inc., 2002. Very technical but very informative; has an amazing style for helping you get the "feel" of a plant.

—. *Herbaceous Perennial Plants.* Athens, GA: Varsity Press, Inc., 1989.

Darke, Rick. *The Encyclopedia of Grasses for Livable Landscapes.* Portland, OR: Timber Press, Inc., 2007. He is both writer and photographer of his own and others' landscapes; a truly impressive work.

Dickey, Page and Hall, John M. *Gardens in the Spirit of Place.* New York, NY: Stewart, Tabori & Chang, 2005. Nice pictures and words about reflective gardens.

DiSabato-Aust, Tracey. *The Well-Designed Mixed Garden.* Portland, OR: Timber Press, Inc., 2003. A thorough and well-organized reference on trees, shrubs, perennials, annuals and bulbs for the garden.

—. *The Well-Tended Perennial Garden: Planting and Pruning Techniques.* Portland, OR: Timber Press, Inc., 1998. The basics on care and maintenance and a whole lot more really good stuff.

Grimsley, Gerrie L. and Young, Jane J. *Contemplative by Design.* Nashville, TN: Upper Room Books, 2008. A very good book of helpful formulas for creating physical settings for contemplation.

Johnson, Hugh. *The Principles of Gardening: the Classic Guide to the Gardener's Art.* New York, NY: Fireside Books, 1987. A reliable classic in the field.

Krymow, Vincensina. *Mary's Flowers: Gardens, Legends, & Meditations.* Cincinnati, OH: St. Anthony Messenger Press, 2002. A very nice Catholic view of it all.

Macunovich, Janet. *Designing Your Gardens and Landscapes: 12 Simple Steps for Successful Planning.* North Adams, MA: Storey Books, 2001. It is about the best book in this genre and an excellent teaching tool.

McDowell, Christopher Forrest and McDowell, Tricia Clark. *The Sanctuary Garden: Creating a Place of Refuge in Your Yard or Garden.* New York, NY: Fireside, 1998. A verbose book with a lot of information on gardening and inspiration.

McGee, Rose Marie Nichols and Stuckey, Maggie. *Bountiful Container.* New York, NY: Workman Publishing Company, Inc., 2002. A wonderful and massive collection of information that can be extended beyond the container garden. One of my favorites.

Midwest Living Magazine, The Healing Garden; an interview with artist Nancy Endres. August 2005, pp. 106-112.

Mosko, Martin Hakubai, Noden, Alse, and Noden, Alxa. *Landscape as Spirit: Creating a Contemplative Garden.* Boston, MA: Weatherhill, Shambhala Publications, Inc., 2005. Contemplative concepts and landscapes with a lot of pictures and, of course, all in perfect balance.

Ogren, Thomas Leo. *Allergy-Free Gardening: The Revolutionary Guide to Healthy Landscaping.* Berkley, CA: Ten Speed Press, 2000. Nicely written with plant listings that are rated by pollen affects on people with allergies.

Realy, Margaret. *Garden Days Lecture Series: Edible Landscaping; How to Create a Potager,* Michigan State University, East Lansing, MI, August, 2008.

—, *Legacy of St. Francis Lecture Series: Annuals and Perennials in the Mixed Border Bed,* St. Francis Retreat Center, DeWitt, MI, March 2005.

—, *Legacy of St. Francis Lecture Series: Creating a Memorial or Prayer Garden,* St. Francis Retreat Center, DeWitt, MI, June, 2008.

—, *Legacy of St. Francis Lecture Series: Easiest Plants to Grow,* St. Francis Retreat Center, DeWitt, MI, February 2007.

—, and Dunbar, Dr. Frank *Legacy of St. Francis Lecture Series: God in the Garden,* St. Francis Retreat Center, DeWitt, MI, March 2006.

Roth, Reverend Nancy. *Organic Prayer: Cultivating Your Relationship with God.* Boston, MA: Cowley Publications, 1993. A very nice and timeless read that will never go out of style as you sit in your prayer garden.

Starr, Mirabai. *Teresa of Avila: The Book of My Life.* Boston, MA: New Seeds Books, 2007. Easy to read; one of my favorite translations. Also available on CD.

Streep, Peg. *Spiritual Gardening: Creating Sacred Space Outdoors.* Maui, HI: Inner Ocean Publishing, Inc., 2003. Excellent resource offering cultural differences in, and types of, spiritual gardens. In my opinion, the best on this subject.

Taylor's Guide, *Gardening Techniques.* Boston, MA: Houghton Mifflin Company, 1991. Like others in this series, this one is reliable and informative.

PHOTOGRAPHS

INDEX

CPSIA information can be obtained
at www.ICGtesting.com
Printed in the USA
BVHW092249050522
636137BV00006B/833